MESSAGES FROM JESUS

"Dearest Mary Ann, I am forever grateful to have experienced your extraordinary presence last February during a Unity service, in Flagstaff, AZ. On that particular Sunday, I was relieved of my childcare responsibilities and was kindly directed into the service. To this day I still reflect back on your words, your singing, your healing abilities and especially your gift of love. You are a gift from God. Never before have my eyes seen so much love radiate from one person.

"In the past, it has been easy for me to be moved by God's greatness through the beauty of nature and Mother Earth, yet not so easy through the sufferings of mankind. However, since you were placed in my life on that memorable Sunday, I can now see God's greatness through human sufferings. I don't know exactly how this happened but you have changed the way I look at life in this physical plane.

"Thank you for finding the energy to write your book; it never leaves my bedside. When my heart can no longer bear to feel the suffering that is all around us, I just think of your special gift of love and know that all is well."

—Blessings to you, Susan Hunter, Flagstaff, AZ

"*Messages from Jesus - A Dialogue of Love* could well be placed on your bookshelf as an extension of the Holy Bible. It keeps pace with the major (and sometimes controversial) subjects and concerns of today's world. Scripture is also brought into clearer focus. Jesus answers questions and offers statements to expand our understanding. All this is recorded and sweetly shared by Mary Ann Johnston. Numerous poems, composed by her, are interspersed throughout the book to either emphasize or become part of the dialogue between herself and Jesus. A most enjoyable bonus!

"Mary Ann, a sincere and highly gifted lady with a lifelong intimacy with Jesus, writes in a most personal way that draws the reader into the message of the book as a participant—not as an outsider who is listening in. The questions she asks of Jesus are often those that we would ask if we were able to do so. The reader will relate to Jesus with a sense that he is speaking to all humanity as well as to Mary Ann. His messages are for all people, for all religions, and for all time."

—Patricia Leach, author, artist, minister
Pasadena, CA

"Dear Mary Ann, Thank you so very, very much for your beautiful book. You truly touched my heart and I am so grateful. . . . Traditional Christianity never reached me, but your beautiful book did. Thank you again."

—B.L
Flagstaff, AZ

"Mary Ann, I really enjoyed your book, *"Messages from Jesus"*. I actually felt a sense of serenity while reading it, but the effect it is having on my wife is profound. She was crying while reading, she said they were tears of joy and gratitude, she felt as if Jesus was in the room with her. She seems to be lighter & happier, like your book flipped a spiritual switch. She has been in great physical pain for some time now and I was wondering if you would see her."

—Take care, John M.
Jenison, MI

"I am reading and re-reading Chapters 5 and 6. It is so intimate, I feel like I am with you in the healing room at your house or on the back patio or sitting at the kitchen table. I am getting so much fuel for meditation, and confidence that—outrageous as my work with the Hunger Project and the activities of my daily life are—I am clearly doing God's work. Thank you so much!!"

—Dorothy Stingley,
Entrepreneur/Activist—Hunger Project
Scottsdale, AZ

Messages from Jesus

A Dialogue of Love

Mary Ann Johnston

Tatienne Publishing
Vanderbilt, Michigan

ORDERS:
http://www.MessagesfromJesus.com
http://www.TatiennePublishing.com
http://www.OutskirtsPress.com/MessagesfromJesus

Johnston, Mary Ann, 1940—

Messages from Jesus: A Dialogue of Love / Mary Ann Johnston.
        1. Religion - Spirituality
        2. Jesus Christ—Apparitions and Miracles.
        3. Spiritual Growth
        4. Christianity

Includes index.
p. cm.

Editor: George O. Johnston

Cover design direction & photography by Linda R. Bayer, RA, of Bayer Essence,
www.bayer-essence.com
Cover Photograph: Sunset over Lake Geneva, in Montreaux, Switzerland

Tatienne Publishing
P.O. Box 326, Vanderbilt, MI 49795

ISBN: 978-0-9817027-5-9

Library of Congress Control Number: 2008941932

Tatienne Publishing and the Tatienne Publishing logo are trademarks belonging to
Tatienne Publishing.

PRINTED IN THE UNITED STATES OF AMERICA

by MARY ANN JOHNSTON

Sustained by Faith – Personal Awakening in God
Messages from Jesus – A Dialogue of Love

CD Hymns of Love

Dedication

This is your book, my friend,
so you can live
Jesus' words of truth and love,
and share them
with others.

"Today, in your world,
you and others are
the voice of God.
True spiritual words are
scripture, even today,
and have the power of
divinity and perfection.
Your writings are filled with
ongoing creative energy
and will not be fruitless.
These words are important and
cannot be stopped."

—Jesus

Contents

Poetry

Acknowledgements

I give thanks for the blessings of God, Jesus and other divine beings, who have continuously strengthened and encouraged me during the writing of this book.

Also, through the efforts of many sweet people, I have been helped in producing this book and making it available. My deepest gratitude goes to:

my devoted husband, whose love, understanding and editing skills were essential in bringing greater clarity to my writing;

Linda Bayer, my daughter, who created the book cover and gives me constant encouragement;

David T. Najdowski, my son, who manages our website;

Song of the Morning Retreat—its peaceful environment, its welcoming people;

my family and many friends and readers who realize revelation is ongoing and that Jesus still speaks to us today.

Author's Note

Song of the Morning is a yoga retreat, nestled deep in the silence and beauty of a Michigan forest. My husband and I built our home in the nurturing space of a new spiritual community here. It is from this peaceful, woodland setting that I write.

Most children lose their ability to see spirit beings or invisible friends. They realize that others can't see them, and they tend to slowly let go of the things grown-ups never saw or have long since forgotten. Or maybe parents and peers tell them how silly they are, so they block out such subtle experiences from their awareness.

As a young child, I was very close to Jesus. He was my invisible friend. All I had to do was think of Him and He would be there and we would communicate through "heart talk" or just be silent. I soon realized that others could not see Jesus and considered me strange when I spoke of our companionship. I loved His nearness and found comfort in His presence, but I learned to keep these experiences to myself. Jesus never faded from my awareness during all my growing up years and as an adult. He continues to be my friend and companion today.

In my openness to the spirit world, I was eventually made aware of having the gift of spiritual healing. I was raised as a conservative Lutheran and did not have much knowledge of such things. I was working as a traveling occupational therapist in hospitals, outpatient clinics and other settings, and the healing ability just appeared. I had a hard time dealing with my new role. I felt separated from my church family. Still, this was not something I could keep secret. This was God's work and could not be set aside.

Then I had a powerful awakening, upon which I became more aware of spirit. I began writing poetry describing my experiences—blissful energies flowing through me, visions of great beauty, deeper understandings, ethereal fragrances, love, oneness. But this awakening separated me even more from those who don't want to hear about things they don't understand. So, I came to live at the Retreat to be able to commune with God and Jesus in an accepting environment. It was here that I met my present husband, who values spiritual matters as I do.

In 2002, Jesus told me I should write books. My relationship with Him was no longer just a personal one. It became all-encompassing and includes all of you who read this dialogue. Jesus is speaking through many others at this time in history and His messages are both timely and timeless. In *Messages from Jesus,* He discusses threats to our health, safety, and environment that didn't exist before. He presents spiritual concepts that few could have understood two thousand years ago. But He also enables us to more fully comprehend the timeless truths He lived and taught at that time. Many people have informed us that this book has given them comfort, hope, and strength for meeting daily challenges, deepened their understanding of truth, answered many of their questions, and helped them be more loving and forgiving.

In *Messages from Jesus*, Jesus often addresses me with the endearments "Saint Ta" or Brave Heart," but even when it seems as if He is speaking just to me, please remember that our dialogue was meant for everyone. Jesus said to me, *"Even if the sharing seems to be concentrated on you, it is not about you. Disown it. Your sharing is about what these writings will do for others."*

So now I share with you what is very sacred to me: my experiences with Jesus and His messages of truth and love.

Chapter One

The Visit

Thou hast given so much to me,
Give one thing more—a grateful heart;
Not thankful when it pleases me,
As if Thy blessings had spare days,
But such a heart whose pulse may be Thy praise.

—George Herbert

One never knows what is going to happen from one moment to the next. One's whole life can change in an instant.

This morning, George, my husband, and I had a disagreement about a person who has a channeling gift and appears to be exploiting it. I argued that he was charging too much for his classes, excluding many people who couldn't afford them. I don't feel exclusivity belongs in the teaching of spirituality. George felt that each of us is on our own path and this person could do as he wanted, just like the rest of us.

Of course George was right, yet I thought my feelings

were justifiable and I was becoming increasingly upset that he did not see things exactly the way I did.

I was about to storm out of the bedroom, when I stopped, turned and emphatically stated, "I can channel Jesus, Yogananda, Sri Yukteswar, Babaji and Sebastian, too!" I had always been skeptical of channeling and my sudden claim startled me. George replied, "Well, why don't you?" I quickly turned and rushed out of our bedroom. I went into the guest bathroom and started to ready myself for our Sunday church service, when, suddenly, there they were, all five of them!

The bathroom took on an expanded dimension. It was no longer the bathroom. Brilliant, white, pulsating light, tinged with faint pastel colors, almost like flames, permeated everything. It was everywhere, as if suddenly a brilliant light had been turned on in the dark. Astounded and awed, I bathed in the light. It filled me.

The masters, in ethereal, yet human form, appeared to be somewhat blended into each other, as if one, and yet separate. A few were elevated off the floor, as if the floor didn't matter. I simply knew who they were. Each appeared to have his own distinct floral fragrance that blended with the others into one exquisite perfume. The aroma penetrated every cell of my body. I could "taste" it in my saliva. My every inhalation, permeated with fragrance, led to a crescendo of unfathomable bliss.

Time had no meaning. My fading argumentative emotions were intermingled with joy. I gasped for breath. . . . Then, in a rush, I said to the masters, "I can't ask you to be here. You have more important things to do."

One of them said, *"All you have to do is say our name or think of us, and believe, and we are there with you."*

The voice was mellow, yet full of power. I suddenly realized I was out of my body! Though I still had conscious awareness, I was not aware of my body. Feeling blissfully calm and in a oneness I cannot put into words, I conversed with the masters in what I call "heart talk."

Contemplatively I said, "So . . . you would be here, anytime, for me to connect with?" I knew in my heart they are always there for me. They must have read my thoughts because they did not acknowledge my question. Increasingly humbled, I continued, "I do have many questions."

Together they answered, *"No. You have many answers."*

In my doubting mind, I did not feel I could provide all the answers. So many things were running through my mind. Thoughtlessly I asked, "So . . . should I put these answers in books or on the Internet, like. . . ?"

Interrupting me, they collectively answered, *"Why not! You would reach more people that way."*

Without thinking, I asked, "Should I charge for this service, too?" At this point they appeared, as one, to be conversing about whatever it was they had in mind for me. It was confusing and I was unable to come to any conclusion. I was feeling left out. They didn't answer my question. Time seemed to simultaneously both speed up and slow down. I was absorbed into their energy, yet I was not given a definite answer.

Suddenly they brought me out of my thoughts, and

seemingly out of context said, *"You should have a new name."*

Immediately, the name "Saint Ta" came to my mind. I reeled from the sudden, unexpected thought of it. Some time ago, one of the masters, Sebastian, had told me "Saint Ta" was a name given to me in a past life for work that I did, an informal name given to me by the local people.

Without giving this name more thought and maybe to change the subject, I asked Jesus, "So . . . what am I to write about?"

"I shall speak to you of love. Before you ask a question, you will have an answer, and the answers will breathe love," replied Jesus.

I turned ever further inward, probing my mind, trying to find answers. I wondered about my ability to write, the significance of sharing revelations from the masters, and what might follow. I asked them, "How am I supposed to do this?"

Then, suddenly, I felt a sense of urgency start to come over me—like a flood—an urgency to write that I could not dismiss. It felt as if the skill to write down the information would simply be there.

While deep in my analytical mind, no longer focused on the masters, I lost them. They left behind a trail of questions that I knew would be answered soon. I knew they would be back. Knowing they are always there for me when I call upon them brings me comfort. For now they were gone.

To have them all come at once was, to say the least, overwhelmingly humbling. The energy was powerful. Time expanded and contracted. As they left and I became lost in thought, I suddenly realized I was back in body consciousness. I felt joy bubbling up inside me. Nearing laughter, I went back into our bedroom and said to George, "You are never going to believe this!"

In the meantime, George had retreated into his bathroom to ready himself for the Sunday service. He told me later he could feel the heaviness of my energy when I stormed out of the bedroom. Then, in my absence, he could feel my energy mellow into a beautiful, calm stillness, unaware of what was happening to me in the other bathroom.

So, when I said to him, "You are never going to believe this," he wasn't surprised. I thank God every day that he is my husband.

All throughout the Sunday service, I was distracted by my thoughts and doubts. I knew I was about to embark on a challenging journey. The responsibilities would be tremendous. My memory had not been very good, following a recent "stroke." I had had very little contact with Yogananda and Sri Yukteswar, and I didn't remember any contact with Babaji* at all. Sebastian was a master from a past life. Jesus has been a part of my life since I was a child.

How could I write books? I tried to meditate and clear

---

* Yogananda, Sri Yukteswar, and Babaji are enlightened beings, who lived in India. At Sri Yukteswar's request, Yogananda came to the United States in 1920 and spread the meditation techniques of India throughout the world. Babaji is an immortal, omnipresent avatar, who has been on earth for hundreds, perhaps thousands, of years. Sebastian has been with Mary Ann, as a teacher and guide, in previous lifetimes and in this life.

my mind. This simply did not work. My mind was too active and full. Many of my thoughts were garbled—just noise. I went over what they had said to me: *"You know that all you have to do is say our name or think of us, and believe, and we are there with you. . . . You have many answers. . . . You would reach more people that way. . . . You should have a new name. . . . Before you ask a question, you will have an answer, and the answers will breathe love. . . ."*

Here I was, faced with what I had always been skeptical of: channeling. And yet this could better be called "superconscious communion" than channeling. The masters did not enter my body and take over my voice. My heart, mind and soul were simply attuned to and uplifted by their blissful, loving presence. I could see them and consciously interact with them on a higher plane than the physical.

One might ask, "How do God, masters, and other spirit beings appear to me? Are they in human form? Are they in color?"

There is no doubt that God is with me always. God is love. God can be found in old people, little children, nature, animals and everywhere in creation. God is one with all, omnipresent.

Sometimes, I feel God's presence as a visual superawareness of divine light, that infuses all things, and everything appears lit up, brighter. The greens are greener, the sky is bluer, and sparkles of light dance in the air. Everything feels alive and I am one with all of it.

Even so, I know I am in the oneness of God even at those times when I am unaware of oneness.

Ever present, Jesus said, *"Even in your unawareness, you are living it. It is like wearing clothing; you are not always aware of the feel of the clothing on your skin, yet it is still there. When you bring your awareness to the clothing, you can always feel it. When you bring your awareness to oneness in God, you experience it."*

"Thank you, Sweet Jesus."

Continuing on . . . Jesus and other masters always come when called upon. Many times they just show up, unannounced. Sometimes I see masters and other spirit beings in ethereal, human form; other times, as ribbons of light, or vast, intense light and color enveloping everything. Beings who have left the earth may have characteristics from their life on earth.

Sometimes masters have come to me without warning, emphatically, and in a rush. Once all the candles that were lit went out. Initially their energy feels overwhelming, and then I feel blissfully calm. With the masters there is often the most heavenly fragrance you could imagine, which permeates every cell of my body. I breathe in the fragrance and can't seem to get enough. All the senses may come into play. Sometimes everything appears to slow down or stand still, for I am passing beyond the physical dimension, which is ruled by time. The pleasure of a master's presence is so beautiful, it sometimes is hard to come back to ordinary consciousness.

I never know how spirits will appear and often don't know when. I feel and sometimes move with profound energies in the area surrounding me. I call this 'dancing with the spirits.' Sometimes I feel their touch and see them.

Sometimes my body or the surrounding air feels extremely cold, or hot, or even heavy. There is a knowing in the presence of spirits. Intuitively, I just know they are there and whether I should acknowledge them or not.

When Jesus, masters and spirits come to me, I am never afraid. If someone comes around a corner and meets me head on, this always startles me, but the sudden appearance of a master or spirit rarely startles me.

Sometimes I sense a spirit who is a lost soul, and I simply talk to it and tell it to go to the light. If it wants to stay, I command it to leave and it does. Occasionally a spirit comes who I immediately know is not there for my best interest. At these times I simply know I am being protected. The presence of God is ever evident to me and, in these instances, even more so. I emphatically command such a spirit to leave in God's name. Occasionally it hangs on. Still I adamantly persist, and within a very short time, it leaves. Sometimes the vision of the spirit is hard to erase from my mind and stays with me for a while, and if I have a hard time dealing with it, then Jesus' face comes into view, taking the place of the spirit every time it comes to mind, and eventually it is forgotten.

I am also aware of a guardian that keeps watch over me. I often smell fragrances of these wonderful guardians, but this one has a foul odor about him. Still I welcome this guardian because I know he is taking care of me.

What do the masters or spirits wear? That is no more important to me than what someone I met at the store was wearing, so I don't always remember. Most often the clothing is as brilliantly illuminated as they are.

How do I communicate with the masters? I use English—usually mental, though sometimes spoken out loud—through heart talk. I call such communication heart talk because it happens with a feeling of great love and from the heart. They talk to me in my language as they would talk to anyone in that person's language, and they use terminology that is appropriate in today's world. Their communication involves more than words or thoughts, for I often feel attuned to so much more. I cannot explain it. I hear a master's voice within my heart and soul, not necessarily through my ears.

How do I communicate with God? I talk to God the same way as with the masters, and I look for God's response in my innermost feelings, outer experiences, nature, and thoughts within me that appear to be coming from God.

Love is what draws me to God and makes communication easy. Through unconditional love—heart, soul, body and mind, filled with the energy of emotion—I feel oneness with God.

"It is this love-generated oneness, the Spirit of God, that connects people to masters and God."

I have been seeing Jesus and spirit beings since I was a small child, so it is natural for me to see them and remain calm. Jesus has always presented Himself to me in a manner that I could understand. God has been good to me. My life has not been easy, but my faith and trust in God brought me from every difficult and wonderful moment to this one. There was never a turning point back to God, because I never lost sight of God.

Can I prove my experiences are real? Probably not, because most people don't have these experiences. I am the one smelling the fragrances, and it has been rare that others could smell them when I do. But I tell only truth, and Jesus' teachings, so full of love and power, speak for themselves.

* * *

I spent most of the day in a daze. My night was spent mainly in prayer. When morning arrived, I was still feeling uncertain about my ability to perform the task ahead of me, yet I knew I needed to start writing. I set up my healing room, lit candles and incense, put on soft music, lay down on the healing table wrapped in a blanket warmed in the clothes dryer, and prayed. I felt comfortable with the realization that I should begin my writing with Jesus. I called on Jesus and told Him I needed to talk to Him, and He was there for me.

"Sweet Jesus, having dialogue with You, and Yogananda, Sebastian, Babaji, and even Sri Yukteswar . . . having dialogue, getting questions answered, and putting it on the Internet or in books makes me feel very strange. It's like exploiting the beautiful words and experiences." Recently someone told me that he wondered how people could possibly share these sorts of things. It seemed sacrilegious to him. At the time, I was unaware that I was going to write books. Remembering that conversation makes me wonder if I would really be doing the right thing.

Breathlessly, hesitantly, I continued, "Oh, Jesus! I know that some things are too sacred to share. Yet in my heart now, I feel an urgency to write, an urgency to share. I don't understand why or how. Help me to do this, Sweet Jesus, without ego getting in the way. Help me to know I am doing the right thing. Keep me from being too elated in this sharing."

"I and my Father are within your heart. We chose you and appointed you, that you should go and bear fruit and that your fruit should abide; so that whatever you ask the Father, He may give it to you. Center yourself and you will not go wrong in your actions. Take time for reflection into your inner true self, as it is given. Your writing is being given a blessing from God."

I momentarily couldn't go on. His beautiful message made me turn inward. There were no feelings or words or actions that could have made any sense. At that moment, I simply "was."

After a space of time I continued, "Sweet Jesus, You tell me writing is a way to reach an audience. Why do I need to reach an audience?"

"Because times are rough. People are afraid."

"Will you give people hope?"

"I will if they listen."

"There will still be a lot of people that this won't reach."

"You will reach a majority."

"Jesus, I have a hard time focusing on philosophical thoughts. Ask George; he'll tell you. Will I really be able to write books?"

"Very definitely."

"One, two . . . ?"

"As many as you wish."

I lost Him at this point. I don't remember any more conversation. It was as if I were falling asleep.

* * *

I wrote down all that had happened to me and then settled back to read it over. It seemed too much to assume a reader would appreciate not one, but five masters showing up in my bathroom. So I discussed this with George and he just listened. I wasn't sure how, but I was determined to leave out that whole scene or parts of it. I thought I might just write about Jesus coming to me and not mention the other four masters or the bathroom. It wouldn't be a lie. Jesus did come to me and I just wouldn't mention the rest.

The following morning, I got up early and, reading what I had written, proceeded to attempt to change it in some way. Suddenly Jesus was standing alongside of my chair, watching, saying nothing. I, too, was doing nothing; I couldn't. My mind was a jumble of nothings. I could not focus on making changes. Once I realized that it had to remain as it was, with all five masters and the setting, Jesus simply faded from my side.

Then I contemplated the name "Saint Ta." I needed to come to terms with this title. When I read back what I had written, up to this point in the text, with concern about the new name, I smelled a strong, beautiful rose fragrance. It seemed to be coming from my hands. Each time I smelled it, I took deep breaths. It was as if I couldn't get enough. Tears came to my eyes. I went into the bedroom to ask George if he could smell the beautiful fragrance. I put my hands up to his nose. He could not smell it. I knew it wasn't lotion or anything I might have handled. When I smelled it, it permeated my whole being. It made me smile and feel blissful. I have had such experiences many times, but every time I do, I am always overwhelmed.

Jesus standing alongside me, preventing me from leaving anything out, and then my smelling the fragrance made me realize even more that everything happening was truth—truth as real as you and I. I was beginning to feel comfortable with my new responsibilities.

Then suddenly a poem came to mind that I had written about Jesus a few years ago.

JESUS' FEET

I stood upon the edge of dawn
And faintly saw a trace of path
Upon the barren desert lawn.
Sand eroded here, a little there,
Brushed aside to make it bare.

I trod upon this path of life
And came upon a bitter hour,
Where I knelt down upon my knees
And, prostrate, fell upon the soil.
I laid my head into my hands,
And sorrow stayed with me the while. . . .

And then I saw, before my eyes,
Dusty, crusted, sandaled feet.
And I looked up into the face.
There was Jesus, King of grace.

Oh . . . breathless . . .
I could barely see for light of Him.
Oh . . . my tongue in mysteries still does sing.
Such wonders of His glorious being!

Upon my knees, I kissed His feet,
Crusted dust and all.
It tasted of sweetness
And smelled of fragrant oil.

Then I hid my face, dissolved my heart;
Through tears of anguish I cried on.

Oh . . . He laid His hands upon my head;
"Walk with me a while," He said.
He led me down my path of life
And has never, never left my side.

I took time out to contemplate the situation and myself.
My thoughts did not always seem to be my own. I
needed more clarity. Part of me wanted the words to just
show up on paper. How would I start? I let days pass. I
hesitated to call upon the masters. I did not feel rushed.

Then very early one morning I felt moved to concentrate on Jesus. First, I prayed to God. "May the words of
my mouth, written words and the meditation of my heart
be acceptable to You, Oh God. Let there be truth. Open
my heart. Open my whole being to Your words. I am

Yours. I give myself to You. Help me to know what is coming from You and what is coming from me."

Jesus appeared when the prayer was finished, as if He had been waiting for it as a catalyst for more dialogue.

"Jesus, recently I said to you that I have so many questions, and You said to me, 'No. You have many answers.' In fact all of you said I have many answers, and yet, I do have many questions."

"Saint Ta, your answers are all within. If you give yourself time and if you think about it, you would find the answers within. The paths you have taken and the journeys you have chosen have brought you to this point. The answers have been within you always, and have lain patiently, awaiting unfoldment."

"I want to be able to give the right answers to everyone. I want them to come directly from Spirit and masters, not from me. I feel they are coming from You, and yet, how can I be sure they are coming from You or God?"

"Remember how it feels when you experience timelessness? In those present moments, all that exists, exists in timeless God-energy. You access all-knowing energy in timeless God-energy. Whether the answers appear to come from you, me, or other masters, they are all God-energy. Calm yourself. Give in to it. Be one with the timelessness. Become the timelessness, the all-knowing, and simply know that Spirit is helping you to access and make known the answers from within yourself."

"How can I be in a state of timelessness all of the time? Is this the same as being in the now, living always in the present moment?"

"The present moment is all there is. You are in the present moment and you are within timelessness: no past and no future, just the present. You simply are. Be yourself."

My thoughts drifted off momentarily. I had grown up with the concept of time as very important. I was always time-conscious.

Continuing on with Jesus, "I experience timelessness often, especially when I go deep into meditation. A few years ago, an experience of timelessness prompted me to write a prose poem. I talked about the in-betweens and the fragrances even back then."

WIND OF CHANGE

Oh, Wind of Change,
you bring with you delight.
I welcome you with open eyes
and mindfulness.

You accuse me of constancy.
I plead innocent.
It was my forefathers and theirs
who inflicted me with this disease of time.

Just try me.
See if I can change.
See if I can open my mind
to expand into no-time.

I have glimpsed the
milliseconds between the milliseconds.
The in-betweens fascinate me.

I have smelled the roses.
I have heard the beckoning.
I have tasted the sweetness of life.
I have been touched by God . . .
and I see the light. . . .

"It is through these prose affirmations that you have received many blessings. Being open to change and growth, and welcoming whatever God wants of you, invites into your life many loving encounters with Spirit."

"Am I writing this book in defiance of . . . ?"

"No."

"This is a big undertaking, Jesus. Will I have the strength and the health to do this?"

"Of course you will."

"About this endearment, 'Saint Ta.' People are going to ask questions about it. I know it's not a canonization; I know that. But, in this day and age, people will question it."

"Use it."

"My daily prayer is asking for freedom from my ego."

"Saint Ta, it is not in your nature to be egotistical. You are too strong for that contrasting delusion. Stop thinking about the ego. Do not give it attention. Free yourself from the hold your earthboundedness has on you. Take on the new person you are daily. Think not of the ego."

A feeling of sheer ecstasy came over me. . . . For a moment in time, all was still. . . . Life stopped. . . . Then, with every inward breath, fragrant energy flowed into the soles of my feet and radiated up, quickly, into all of my body and out my crown. The more deeply I inhaled, the stronger the energy became. I couldn't get enough of it. I could taste the fragrant sweetness of it. It lingered long within. . . . I felt heady. . . . My breathing became as if nothing but pure rose fragrance.

"SAINT TA," Jesus' words reverberated in my very being, shaking me somewhat from the bliss. *"This fragrance is given to you as a sign to affirm authentication of our presence and, further, a consent for you to use the title 'Saint Ta.' You are born again into a new life daily, and today is special."*

Time passed or was it the next instant that I again remembered something I had written about the divine breath. It seems strange to me that these conversations would prompt me to remember prose and poetry that I had written in the past. What was happening? Was I preparing for this way back then?

BREATH OF GOD

The evening floods the space.
With quiet thoughts I spend
the time alone in all the splendor here.
The breath of God is felt
upon my brow.
I gasp and hold. . . .

Eternity comes . . . is spent.
Then I let the vapor go
upon the streamers of the deep,
who hold the answers so.

The breath then comes again . . .
caressing me within
from crown to feet
and back again to heart.
I let it go right in,
then aim it out to you
to mend and love,
and love and mend,
and mend and love again.

The breath comes once again . . .
from me to you
and you to me,
going deep within, without,
healing what has been and is,
and letting go of that.

> Memories . . . speculations . . .
> The moment is
> where I am. . . .
> I jump into the midst of it.

I felt as if Jesus was trying to wake me from a long slumber. After a moment of collecting myself, I went on.

"Jesus, I wish I could preserve everything that You tell me. A lot of it is throughout the day and it's little tidbits, here and there. I can't carry my recorder around with me all the time and my memory is so short. I don't remember all these conversations unless I record them, type them, or tell them immediately to George. And then, later on, he is able to help me remember. All my life You have listened to me and I to You. And yet, I wonder why I can't remember these conversations. They are so significant and so beautiful. And there are so many of them. Why is it that I can't remember all of them? Is it because of my past stroke?"

"You did not have a stroke. You had an awakening."

"I had stroke symptoms, but they couldn't find a cause, except for an increase in the megahertz of brain activity."

"Saint Ta, you had an awakening that connected you to your higher creative power and higher realization of God's graces by expanding your brain activity to higher dimensions of wakefulness."

I'll never forget that New Year's Day in 1998.

Upon awakening, early that morning, my pelvic floor clamped shut, containing in me a pulsating, flowing energy that spread quickly up my spine, out into my limbs and into my head, as if I were a vessel to be filled then emptied, again and again.

I surrendered to its awesome intensity, as every energy-filled breath built upon each preceding breath. Still there was no fear, just an all-pervading, blissful calmness, and I went where sound does not exist and time is unknown. Finally, as it flowed from me, it took more than I had to give, leaving me partially paralyzed.

During many months of rehabilitation and healing, I became increasingly aware of divine oneness and beauty and wrote poems about the sacred experiences I was having.

I realize now that this spiritual awakening prepared me for writing this book with Jesus and sharing His messages with others. I asked Him, "Why me? The 'stroke' did have its toll on my memory."

"Why not you? . . . You hold conversations with Spirit all the time, whether it is verbal or mental. It is in your nature to be open to Spirit. You live in Spirit. What is revealed to you is for the present, and the rest is safe, within your body, mind and soul, waiting to be remembered when you need it.

"Share only what you remember. Do not worry about things forgotten. We want you to reach those whom the messages will inspire and give comfort. My words and the words of the Father abide in you. We will be here to help you and guide you. Share your memories."

"It would be so much easier if I could remember more."

"Saint Ta, your mind, to you, seems slower now for re-

membering. You don't realize you are still taking in information—information you are not even aware of. Your brain is expanding for things spiritual. You and many others have been doing things in your awake and sleep state that most people don't even dream of and even you aren't always conscious of. Only your outer self knows of all these things. During the day, during your conscious dream world, you think you should remember all things, and for you, Saint Ta, you need to live in the present remembering moment and only share what you remember and are moved to share.

"Renew yourself daily in your breath work. In that, you find rest and healing. Do not concern yourself over hidden memories. Share remembrances."

"You said that memories are stored within the body, mind, and soul, and now you say only the outer self knows of all these things. What do you mean?"

"If you were to go deep into meditation, within, you would find your outer self—the soul. In that state of consciousness, the physical body disappears and simply does not exist. It is within this consciousness that you and others are able to tolerate the collective condition of the earth while bringing light into the world. Since this is egoless action, it is rarely brought to memory in the physical consciousness."

"If I only live in the present—no past, no future—how can I share remembrances? I don't understand."

"Living in the present moment enables you to see only

what is before you without comparisons. You must live in the present moment with love and with no concern over the past or the future of self and others. These present moments filled with love can only build beautiful memories. There would never be anything negative to compare and to judge from the past, if all humans lived each and every present moment lovingly.

"Yes, there would be past remembrances; however, memories would soon be filled with a past of love without judgment. Therein would be all the remembrances to share with others in the present.

"And too, you are opening up more and more to remembering God. Above all, share this remembrance."

I smiled within. A comforting feeling came over me. All felt well.

"Jesus, I received a message recently. Seemingly, it came from all of you. The message went at a very brisk pace. It said, 'Jesus will converse with you about love. Yogananda will converse with you about meditation. Sri Yukteswar will converse with you about discipline. Sebastian will converse with you about service. And that is all the message said, yet, in the beginning of this whole thing, Babaji was present too. I wonder about Babaji. What is he going to talk to me about?"

"Babaji will have to speak for himself."

"Babaji only spoke to me once, only once that I remember."

"Only once that you know of."

Suddenly, a corner of my mind veil lifted and revealed Babaji himself! Amazingly, I felt at ease as I sat in this still space of time with Babaji. I remember the overwhelming stillness. Only one transmission took place that I can remember. Just before leaving me, Babaji told me what he is going to discuss with me: manifestation. I did not flinch. I felt very calm. I accepted what he said without question. Smiling, I mentally lowered the veil. . . .

After a time of meditation, I slowly started having thoughts about how little I know about manifestation and especially about Babaji. Yet I have a feeling I know more than I think, now that I have been lost in time with Babaji.

I suppose some of you would like to know what Babaji looked like. All I can say is he was like joy immemorial. Playful and ever changing, youthful to aged. I don't remember much more than that.

"So many people believe that their master is the one and only. How will they possibly understand and believe all that You and the other masters tell them?"

"God would not have given you the gift for healing if He had thought you would be weak in the face of unbelievers. The healings were not always understood by others, and yet, the healings were tangible and able to be seen. You were able to overlook the unbelievers and carried on. Blessed are those who do not see or hear and yet believe. Do not worry yourself over others' disbelief.

"God did not send masters for this age only. In the minds of many they limit God. God is limitless. There have been other Christed avatars and many true masters in different regions of your earth. Those who feel their avatar or

master is the one and only have caused unrest and wars throughout your world. Their inability to accept the fact that each of you is entitled to have your own master and teacher is detrimental to all organized world religions. They don't realize that having the same God is what binds them together.

"And now we have appointed you to reach out to those who will listen."

"It wasn't until a few years ago that I was able to acknowledge that other masters even existed. You have always been my master.

"From childhood, in Sunday School, I was taught to take my problems to You, Jesus, and to talk with You. I have done that. As a child I listened. As an adult I still listen. The listening has never been taken away from me as it has for others. When it comes down to it, people simply don't remember that part of their heritage—the listening part."

"Many take their problems as far as telling to and asking of God or teacher, but they don't often listen because they don't believe they will hear an answer, or they don't take the time to meditate. The world has taken the creative mind out of the child at a very young age. Their creativity has been stymied by environment, parents, teachers, television and even siblings. They do not know how to listen to Spirit and nature and their own intuition anymore."

"That's the part people will question—my being able to listen to You and other masters and saints. I guess I want everyone to be able to believe as I do."

"Just know I and my Father will be there for those who want to listen and are open and believe."

"And what of the other masters and saints?"

"We are all one in Spirit. Your beliefs have made you whole."

"What do you mean by 'whole'?"

"Your unwavering beliefs have led you to your awakening. You have been made whole through this process. Further, your awakening has made you ever-more aware of your creative ability to heal, and to connect with the masters and spirits and anyone else you might call upon to aid you in your work."

"Is it possible that others do not know what they should be listening for?"

"God said, 'Be still and know that I am God.' Tell them, 'God is in the stillness. Go within. Center yourself in meditative quietness. When you can let go and quiet yourself, you will become aware of the loving presence of God in all things, everywhere, and you will realize oneness with God, or Spirit. If you imagine you are hearing God, you are hearing God. If you imagine you are hearing a master, you are hearing a master. Answers may come to you before you even ask a question. Simply listen.'

"Saint Ta, it is with honor that we communicate with you. We love you."

Catching my breath at His words, I said, "Oh . . . my dear Lord, it is my honor to be in Your presence. . . . Thank you for your loving patience with me.

"Even though I am typing these conversations with You, Jesus, I also have had conversations with some of the other masters, but I haven't been typing them. And then I am forgetting what occurred. . . ."

"When it comes time to focus on one of the others for your books, you will remember many wonderful, important things to write about. Do not worry. Right now, just think love. You are worrying too much. All in due time."

I stopped a moment. Looking out our windows, morning had leisurely arrived. Nature and I were wide-awake. I took a deep cleansing breath and centered myself. The early mornings with Jesus are so beautiful and it gives me a deep inner peace. Calmly I continued, "There are so many books written now about God and the masters, is there really a need for more?"

"Many wonderful people are writing books about their experiences with God and masters, each addressing different needs for the many different people, each written in different ways to address the different ways people learn and respond to teachings."

"Are they all genuine?"

"Books are genuine when they are based on truth and love. Yet I tell you, you will not find God in books. Books can only help steer one toward divine inner creativity and self-realization. Books of truth are stepping-stones on the soul's journey. And you will know a book of truth by how it resonates within you.

"Still, if it is a true teaching and you are uncomfortable with it, you may simply not recognize it or be ready for it.

"We want you to write so that children will be able to understand our messages."

"Children? . . ."

"Adults fill their minds full of intellectual theory they don't need to know. They often miss the simple truths when they are unable to be as creative as a child. You must speak to the adult child, too. Write books that will reopen inner creativity within all the children of God—all ages, young and old—so they will more easily understand our messages of love."

"Then I must write this simply, so all will understand."

"Always do all things simply, with love. You will be inspired to write so others will be able to remember their creativity."

"You mentioned that I should simply listen, and answers would come before the questions. Yet, here I am, asking complete questions, and you are answering them. And yet, sometimes the answers are there before the questions come."

"The answers are there before you ask a question because you have all the answers within. However, we will be there for you, to guide and assist you in writing these messages for all people everywhere."

"Will we address new topics never discussed before? Will there be new revelations?"

"No. All made known to you is known in the past-present-future. Mankind has not always listened to God. Masters have been sent with messages that were often misunderstood. Books have been inspired and not read. Visions have been disbelieved. Therefore, my messages will seem new to many people. They may even seem new to you, Saint Ta. Even now, there will be unbelievers."

I felt like a great task was set before me. It seemed more than I could do. Overwhelmed, I thought about what was ahead of me. How could I explain all of this to my family and friends? Would they understand my having a new name? I didn't want them calling me "Saint Ta."

Hesitantly I said, "I am honored by your beautiful presence, Sweet Jesus." Hurriedly I continued, "But I can't help feeling that I don't want everyone calling me 'Saint Ta.' I would feel too uncomfortable."

"We wanted to honor you with a name, and 'Saint Ta' was what came to your mind. It was the right answer."

"You mean this was my idea? 'Saint Ta' was my idea?!"

"It is an honor given from masters or teachers to their disciples. Many of my disciples you read about in the Bible had new names bestowed upon them during their discipleship. It is not an unusual thing to do. We wanted someone to write the books so that children could understand them. When you were Saint Ta in the past, you helped abandoned and ill children. We think of you often, lovingly, as Saint Ta, and we wanted to honor you with your forgotten name."

Dizzily rattling on, I said, "I am honored, however, I still have misgivings about using the word 'Saint.' It will appear to be an ego trip, and I don't want that. What if I just use 'Ta' without the 'Saint'? . . ."

"YE ARE ALL SAINTS!!"

The words slammed through my body like a kundalini of lightning and thunder, shaking me to my roots. Tears came . . . flowed. . . . I would have fallen if I hadn't already been sitting. There was no anger in the words, just divine power. They filled me. . . . Time passed, or stood still; I don't know which. Still in a nearly-electrified, disoriented trance, I slowly started to gain steadiness. Taking a deep breath, I calmed myself. . . . Overcome by the omnipotence of the words, I became increasingly humbled in realizing the honor that was given me, and I was ashamed of my doubting.

Chapter Two

God and the Masters

"In reality, there are as many religions as individuals."

—Mahatma Gandhi

Often, in this winter wonderland, a patch of blue-sky opens up and sunlight streams down. Lighting up the forest, the sun turns snowflakes on the heavily-laden pine boughs into sparkling gems.

Our quiet, wintry days are spent in meditation, healing, counseling, writing and planning for the busy seasons ahead. I don't feel pressed into talking with Jesus or other masters. It does not require effort. It happens naturally. And then . . .

"Sweet Jesus, how would I know a true master?"

"By the obvious divinity permeating the master's loving nature."

"I thought there was divinity in everyone."

"Yes. God is within all. There is divinity in all."

"Then that would make us all masters?"

"All on earth have potential to be masters but must first awaken to their divine intuitive powers of creation. To remember your divinity you must be able to be aware of the omnipresence of God in all creation, even unto the ends of the universes, and to live in love at all times, in non-judgment, as one with all, while administering to the needs of others.

"A master dwells, and continues to grow, in the oneness of God and loves unconditionally and without ego. This is what the average human aspires to be also."

"How can we tell a false master?"

"The false master may have an inflated, egotistical charisma that will charm you or entrance you into conformability, and/or may take advantage of you in non-loving ways. Be aware of the false master, for, as such, they may appear to be teaching true righteousness, and yet they will be unable to live in the loving oneness of God at all times. They will not be truth."

"In Romans 8:14, Paul says, 'For all who are led by the Spirit of God are sons of God.' Does this mean that we, as normal humans, could become sons of God?"

"All who set their mind on God and live in the Spirit are sons of God. Even my Lord's Prayer, as you know it, addresses God as the Father. Does that not make you sons and daughters?"

"I like to address my prayers to God as 'Heavenly Father, Divine Mother'. . . ."

"That makes you a daughter." At this He smiled.

"Is there a difference between You, as 'the only begotten Son', and the rest of us, as sons and daughters?"

"Let me explain so that you will understand. The Father created all things visible and invisible including the Son, which is the Christ Consciousness, out of which are born Christed avatars to aid humanity. The Father also created the omnipresent Spirit, which lovingly sustains all within creation. Father, Son as Christ Consciousness and Holy Spirit are all One.

"The term 'Christ Consciousness' is more recent than of old and yet is a good expression of the meaning of 'the only begotten Son of God.'

"The term 'Christ' goes further back than biblical times. Krishna, as a Christ, lived three thousand of earth's years before me. There were others before and since, all highly-evolved, fully-realized beings. Dogma has distorted the true meaning of Christ, limiting God, once again, to one Christ. God cannot be limited.

"I, Jesus, a Christ given out of the Christ Consciousness, contain the Father, and the Father contains the Son, and the Spirit of God contains the Father and the Son, and the Father and the Son contain the Spirit. All beings in one, beyond duality, are also within the Son of God, or Christ Consciousness. However, it is only a few who, as highly-evolved, realized avatars, are chosen to be saviors of this world and the next. I am in each of you, and you are in me, and we are in the Father, the Son, and the Spirit. All abide in love, in Christ Consciousness, as one.

"Yet it is more deep than what you have ever imagined. There are mysteries that will not be revealed to anyone on this earth plane. Within your dualistic world, oneness is difficult for most humans to experience. I can only will that you understand what I have said."

"Well . . . let me try to reiterate here. All beings are in one, but only some of them are fully aware of this oneness. Those who are, realize Christ Consciousness. The rest of humanity, even though they are in one, do not yet fully experience this oneness.

"Thank you, Saint Ta. You are right."

"Are most of us different from Christed avatars only because of a lack of awareness of our oneness?"

"If that were so, there would be an abundance of avatars, and mankind would rely on avatars instead of their own selves for personal and spiritual growth, as so often happens when people rely too much on masters and clergy. What is learned from living on earth has a direct effect on your growth and karma."

"How are avatars different from the rest of humanity?"

"Avatars are different from humanity in that they naturally love, serve, and play in the oneness of all creation and never lose sight of this awareness, even with distraction and difficult circumstances. In their heart they know they are avatars, yet have no ego attachment to this designation. An avatar is never boastful, nor would an avatar lay claim to fame. You might know someone who appears to be as an avatar, and that may be rightly so; however, avatars are

chosen by God, when God intervenes for the sake of all mankind and creation. An avatar may not only be visible on earth, but may have other duties elsewhere.

"Humans are just that, human. Humans have many of the characteristics of avatars but are not able to release the ego and maintain love for all creation at all times."

I was out of focus and nearly disoriented from all that was said. Only by going within was I able to quiet my restlessness. Time passed or stood still; I don't know which. Then I read it again.

Continuing on, I asked, "How will we recognize an avatar?"

"An avatar is a Christed incarnation of God, not as a whole of God because of the limitations of the body, but as an element of God, given out of the Christ Consciousness. An avatar knows, from birth or from the time of choosing, that he or she is an avatar and where their path will lead. All avatars are also masters, but not all masters are avatars.

"An avatar has power to perform miracles. However, it will not be only miracles that will help you to recognize an avatar. The gift of healing has been given to many. Avatars often have specific tasks to perform, with messages for humanity, and so, therefore, may be reclusive until they are ready to be found.

"Still, Christed avatars have free will and are challenged by many trials and may fall from grace. Woe to those who claim to be a Christed avatar or master and are not truth. And woe to those who, even in their knowing they

are not a Christed avatar or master, allow others to believe so."

"I went to see Ammachi. She is a saintly person who gives blessings to thousands of people through her blissful hugs. Is she an avatar?"

"That is not for me to divulge."

"I sometimes feel her in pain. I send healing for her highest good, always with the will of God in mind as I pray. It feels right to do so, and yet, am I assuming too much here: that I, a simple human, could in fact eliminate the pain of a saintly person such as Ammachi through God's healing grace?"

Laughing, Jesus replied, *"Saint Ta, you are not a simple human. No one is. Even I asked my disciples to pray for and with me. Prayer never goes unanswered. Wipe away your doubts."*

"Sweet Jesus, why are there so many different pictures of You? People see You in so many different ways."

"It is how mankind would imagine I would look or how they actually see me. Or they might have seen a comforting picture of me when they were children and that image stayed with them. To some, I am a strong, muscular type. To others, I am tall and thin. To some, I am dark and, to others, light. I enjoy the diverse images of myself that people come up with. It, especially, brings me great love and joy when children draw me!"

"I would love to take brush and paint to do portraits of

masters, but I don't think that will happen. I am not a painter. Many of the pictures of You, Jesus, depict facial features and even skin color that are different from what I see. I don't feel the need to paint You, yet I was once asked to write a poem about You, Jesus, as a clown!"

JESUS IN THERE

Under confines of costume,
Face paint and frizzy hair,
There's a person in there.

Within the guise
Of expressive eyes
That accept your stares,
There's a person in there.

Behind the act
Of fiction or fact,
Performance with flair,
There's a person in there.

From the heart
A story to share,
Life's play revealed.
Could be Jesus in there.

Lifting despair,
Softening hurts,
Quieting minds.
Surely Jesus in there.

"I stand behind every clown that ever brought happiness to humanity. Laughter promotes love, joy, forgiveness, and releases fears and pain. If only humans could laugh more."

"I often see you amused."

"I am easily amused. With joy, l laugh when children and you laugh. And, with happiness, I laugh when any of creation laughs."

"Some say you do not laugh."

"Laughter, joy, sadness and all emotions are one in love. Still, within the earth plane, most of mankind experiences emotions as separate and not as one. I, as an omnipresent Son of God in Christ Consciousness, am here for all of mankind. And in this earth plane I, too, enjoy separate emotions, so that I can truly and lovingly address all personal and collective experiences and you can relate to me. How could you relate to me if I were of one emotion, love, until you understand oneness? Through my omnipresence I am all things to all people.

"And it doesn't matter how I look. That is not important. I am in every portrait of me that ever was. Again I say, I, in Christ Consciousness omnipresence, am all things to all people.

"Most important are the messages that I bring to humanity: God is a loving God. Live in love with all of creation in non-judgment, forgiving yourself and all others, and sin no more. This is the truth, and in this way of living, your past sins are released and none are made."

"Do you mean to say that we really can forgive our own sins?"

"Yes."

"Why do we still feel like we have to be forgiven?"

"Humans are very hard on their selves. For so long as you do not forgive yourself and others for what you perceive as sin, you will continue to address it through karma. For you create your own path. There is no need for karmic debt. Forgive the past of self and others, and live each present moment in love, and sin no more."

"Ah, that is the catch. 'Forgive, and sin no more.' Yet, we continue to reinvent karmic debt by continuing our sinful ways without forgiveness. Does God forgive our sins daily?"

"God is a loving God. God does not judge. God may intervene to make change in your life and others', but God does not judge. Mankind must be forgiving, so no karmic debt is created. If people truly forgave their selves and others, they would be so full of light it would feel as if the weight of the world was lifted from them. They would simply sin no more."

"I know people who go to confession and come out forgiven and then continue their old pattern of wrongdoings."

"Saint Ta, it is not like you to judge."

"Sorry. I have been trying hard to overcome my judgmental nature. It's not easy. I find myself comparing and criticizing sometimes. I am trying to think about what I am thinking. It helps."

"Forgive yourself daily and start over. All you who con-

tinue your judgmental ways know you are doing so. You are only deceiving yourselves. You are creating your own life and karma, and what you sow you reap. If it seems overwhelming to change your sinful ways, practice forgiveness of yourself for one thing at a time. Practice discernment with non-judgment, and practice forgiving one other person at a time."

"I remember reading somewhere that it takes thirty days in a row, practicing something new, to make it a habit. I tried this when I had to start wearing seat belts. I didn't want to wear one. I decided, since it was something I had to do, I would do what the article said and practice doing it for thirty days. I disciplined myself into doing it every time I got in the car. It was, in fact, a habit by the time the end of the thirty days came. So bad habits can be broken and we can learn new ways."

"Yes, habits can be broken with choice and discipline. New beliefs can be learned, and old beliefs can be forgotten."

"In the Bible, God was a vengeful, judgmental God, and now has changed into a loving God. Why did God change?"

"God did not change. God has always been a loving God. The ancients needed a vengeful god to survive. They were living in times of mass disorder. Their perceived God-given punishments were harsh, for what they sowed they reaped. It appeared to them that a vengeful God was punishing them. However, it was they, who were so unforgiving

of self and others, that they were doing the punishing, set-
ting people against people and then giving God credit for
the punishments they received in turn. Ancient historians
and prophets wrote of this vengeful God. Even today, God
is portrayed as vengeful in many religions around your
earth."

"Are you saying the ancient prophets were wrong?"

"No. There was indeed a vengeful God, for what man-
kind perceives they create. They needed a God to keep or-
der, and within and among them, they created a vengeful
God. Mankind still does this today. But I tell you, God is
truly a loving God. Look about you. Does not the eternal
rising and setting sun tell you of a loving God? Does not
the warmth of a child or the passing of the seasons tell you
of a loving God?

"Yet even I have talked of a day of judgment. On that
day the Son of God, Christ Consciousness, will make truths
known to you. Your life will lie open before you. With your
free will, you will be the judge. All of your life you have
been hard on yourselves. So, too, on judgment day."

"I am not eloquent in my writings, nor am I able to put
words to my thoughts very well. But I want to reiterate here
to see if I am understanding this correctly."

"Ah, Saint Ta, your words are my words and the words
of the Father. You are being led in your questioning."

"I think You are saying that when we pass over, it is the
Christ Consciousness within each of us who would make us
aware of the sins we might not have even realized were

sins, and then we self-judge. Terrorists who feel they are doing the right thing come to my mind."

"You understood that correctly. It is, however, not for you to judge terrorists. It is up to the law of the land, and finally, through death and destiny, truths will be made known to the terrorist and they will be judged by self with God's discerning intervention."

I stopped and looked out the windows. I felt cold. The fire in the wood stove was nearly out. I set it ablaze once more. Feeling warmer, I sat back down and looked up and gazed into a blue patch of sky. I felt riveted into its depth, almost as if it were calling me. Mesmerized, I felt dizzy. I had to force myself away from it. I meditated for a while. In those moments, I understood so much more than what He said.

"Sweet Jesus, why aren't there more acknowledged masters?"

"There are many awakened masters, male and female. They do not always seek acknowledgment. You may not find them readily. Some have chosen to be on earth as well as performing higher duties. They do not hide, but they often live in quiet, reclusive settings. Seek them out. They have much to give and teach.

"There are also masters among dense populations. They have a God-filled reserve within, that permeates their being to sustain them as they work, even in the most trying of human conditions. You will recognize them by their egoless, self-sacrificial, good deeds, humbly performed in the midst

of love and chaos."

"Why do we need other masters as well as Yourself? We have You, and yet, there are other masters we have heard about, some alive and some passed on. But it seems one would be enough."

"You are each unique in your spiritual growth. You come from different countries and backgrounds, with different parental guidance. Religion is often a learned experience because everyone else is doing it, so too, do you follow their master. It is important that masters and teachings are there for the many different cultures, just as there are many books with the same messages to address the many different peoples. All true masters are one and worship the same God.

"And yet, I tell you, you do not need an avatar or a master or a saint to bring you to enlightenment. God is within . . . enlightenment is within. Where God is, enlightenment is. Go there, in love, and be made whole."

"Are you saying we don't need a teacher of any kind to achieve God-realization?"

"Those who seemingly never heard of God or masters, and yet have lived in love, are experiencing spiritual progress by finding God through their exposure to nature and life experiences. A master or guru or teacher will be acknowledged by the person only when needed.

"Those who rely on a living teacher, guru, or saintly master experience spiritual progress, as do those who have no more need for teachers. Then there are those who wor-

ship masters who have passed on.

"All mankind has experiences to help them become aware of their enlightenment within . . . their divinity within. All is already all one. Each lifetime builds upon the previous lifetime, and all paths end in the final resting place, with God in love.

"Emerson wrote, 'One rose makes no reference to former or better roses. They are for what they are. They exist with God today. There is no time for them. There is simply the rose. It is perfect in every moment of its existence.'"

Astonished, I asked, "You mean Emerson, the American poet? You read Emerson?"

"Read? Well, yes, and with admiration."

Amused, I continued, "So You are saying we don't need teachers or masters. That God, as teacher, is enough."

"If you need a teacher, you will know and your true teacher will appear. I simply wanted to express to you that some people have reached a time when they could set teachers aside to be with God in all they do. One way is not better than another way. Read the reference of the rose again, out loud."

Out loud I read, "One rose makes no reference to former or better roses. They are for what they are. They exist with God today. There is no time for them. There is simply the rose. It is perfect in every moment of its existence."

"That is beautiful. It speaks of non-comparison and of timelessness in the present moment. It says it all."

"Yes, it does."

Momentarily, I thought about the roses as people. I sat and meditated for a while.

"One path is not better than another, as they are all one. All lead to God. Everyone imagines they are on a different path but, ultimately, they all have the same destination: God-realization, heaven. Just as there are many roads to any one city, there are many ways to get to God, none better than another. Some paths are higher, but that doesn't make it better."

"What makes one path higher than another?"

"Higher means only that a person is nearer to God-realization than another. Still there is no comparison. The closer one gets to God-realization, the more intense the desire to experience divine bliss. And in this desire they live more fully in God. This does not mean it is better than another path, just closer to fulfilling where all paths lead. All paths eventually lead to God."

"When I sold my home and we made ready to build, spirit told me to 'sell, buy, and move in.' Spirit did not say we should build. I felt this had something to do with my health. Whether that was God talking or a master or my own intuition, I am not sure. My memory does not serve me well here.

"Contrary to what was implied, we did build in this beautiful retreat. It was extremely hard, this building process. And yes, I can see where it could have been damaging to my health more than it was. However, the peaceful, yet powerful energy in this wonderful retreat has afforded both of us the ability to sustain our health and to be of service to the many people who find their way to our doorstep and the Retreat. I did not follow spirit-guidance and yet I am happy here.

"After we had moved into our home, Sebastian told me, 'You took a higher path.' I did not understand the meaning until now. So am I correct in assuming that buying a home elsewhere would have slowed our spiritual path?"

"In the Retreat, you are granted the solace that you wanted for your spiritual growth. It does not mean this path you chose was the only way. This is not to be for everyone. Others choose different paths to the same goal, no better or worse than your chosen path. Growth will come to all.

"You have set a precedence in your spiritual community that has helped others. This is a part of your and George's higher path, to set an example for present and future inhabitants in your community and for those you reach in these writings."

"Ah, Sweet Jesus . . . so many people talk of your return. How are we to recognize this when it happens?"

"Saint Ta, you and many others have experienced my return, as if I have never left you. You are blessed. Yet many others are still awaiting my return, and still others are unaware. I tell you that I come, in Christ Consciousness, like a thief in the night. I have been there for each of you, many times, and you have not recognized me. There was and is no warning. Be prepared at all times.

"Yet, when I return for all of mankind, all shall know. I cannot tell you when this will be. Only my Father can tell

us. If I could tell you the hour or day, you would wait to prepare for that day.

"Be wary of all those who claim to be Christ. For unless this Christ comes with the highest heavens and all of nature rejoicing, he will not be truth.

"I will come, in Christ Consciousness, for all people everywhere, with the glory of the heavens and earth, and all on earth shall know. There will be no doubt."

"Will the kingdom of God be revealed to us?"

"Behold the kingdom of God is within and in the midst of you. It is in every breath you take."

I was becoming increasingly filled with the breath of God. I had to stop and lie down. I felt catatonic, as if imprisoned, in an embrace of high ecstasy.

Chapter Three

Love

Love never ends . . .

—1 Corinthians (13:8)

We are in the dead of winter. Strange terminology, isn't it? Winter is far from dead. Still and quiet, yes, but not dead. The energies here at the Retreat are every bit as powerful in the winter as at any other time of the year. Guests still brave the snow and ice, even in the harshest of weather.

Some newcomers find they cannot tolerate the solitude for very long. They say they want to be here, but the silent nature of the Retreat is difficult to face, so they often cut their visit short. Many come back, gradually increasing the length of their visits.

Ever present, Jesus said, *"Ah, reluctant, yet still-searching, hearts! Your world is making you who you are, instead of allowing your own true selves become who you are. You must learn to give in to your quiet inner selves, even in the outer world."*

"When retreatants come to Song of the Morning, they often ask, "How can I stay quieted and peaceful when I must consider the world and family?"

"There are no hard and fast guides on how to access inner peace, only generalities. No one can set specific guides to meet all people's needs. Not everyone is ready. Each person is at a different place within their spiritual growth. You must first make up your mind to become the change you want for yourself, and then take charge of your life.

"You often think you don't have the time to sort it out. You limit yourselves from the most important things."

"Often they tell me they can't live a quiet life because of all their responsibilities at home or work, and they don't have time for solitude."

"Think on this. If you are unable to have quiet time during your day, practice wakeful meditation in your busy life. In this wakeful meditation, go about your duties and encounters with love. Imagine each moment as the only moment, because it is. Live, knowing you are in the presence of God. Meld lovingly into all situations—into all people, children, nature and even material things.

"Living in the presence of God in each and every present moment brings harmony, and you begin to feel inner peace and oneness with all that is, even in your busiest times. Each and every one of you is worthy of inner peace, a gift freely given to you from God. It is vital for your well-being."

"I am aware of the oneness of all as I live my daily life,

and I am loving in all that I do and say. Yet I find that it is hard to hold onto that thought when things are rough or I am not feeling well. It seems to be getting easier and easier, but I am not always feeling loving."

"Saint Ta, that is a beautiful affirmation: 'I am aware of the oneness of all as I live my daily life and I am loving in all that I do and say.' I only ask that you practice these things. Unconditional love will come easier and easier if you practice, practice, practice."

"Thank You, Sweet Jesus, for all that you give and teach."

"It is in the act of giving that you receive. All people receive what they give. If you give love, you receive love. If you give hurt, sadness and judgment, you will receive like gifts."

"You would call hurt, sadness and judgment gifts?"

"These gifts are lessons, and all lessons are gifts. These seemingly unharmonious lessons enable you to realize your faults."

"What if I choose not to acknowledge my faults?"

"You create your own world. It is in your giving that you receive, and you will receive. You will be presented with your faults through lessons, in many ways, until you realize these faults must be acknowledged and not repeated. If you do not attend to your faults, they will simply come back to you, even in the hereafter, for as you sow, you reap.

"In like manner, the love you give will be returned to you in many ways."

"Who gives these lessons? If I am not aware of my faults, how can I know what it is I am doing wrong?"

"Your inner and outer self knows of your faults and makes you aware of your wrongdoings through lessons. The ego makes you aware of what you need to work on. Pay attention to your ego. Does your ego make you arrogant? Then work on arrogance. Does your ego make you feel better than others? Then work on non-judgment.

"You must quiet yourself and ask how you can improve yourself. Answers come in lessons: as spoken words from God, master, or others, as written words, as true intuition, and sometimes in harsh realities. Be ever mindful of what you are doing and creating.

"As you learn to acknowledge your faults and choose to learn from them, your spiritual path becomes narrower."

"What do You mean, narrower?"

"Living in love makes it easier to recognize your faults, and you begin to learn from them. Your attention grows more and more focused on only good, and you notice less and less distractions. This makes for a narrower path, making it easier to be aware of God in your life. This does not mean you have a narrower field of experience; it simply means that you are more focused and will not be easily distracted on your spiritual path."

"I feel my life is so much richer and more meaningful with God as my focus. I love my time with God when I meditate during my day."

"As you begin to live in love and feel the presence of God in your life, you will long for ever-more ways to quiet your inner self. Retreats provide a place to fulfill your longing to know God, whether it is at Song of the Morning, or sitting on the beach of a great ocean or in a chosen corner of your home for meditation. A retreat takes you away from all the distractions that are prevalent in the world today. Once this desire to know God is kindled, you will long for more solitude for inner reflection, for God can be found within you. Just simply know that God is within you."

"Some tell me there is no place for solitude in their homes, out of reach of small children. I can believe that. I've been there. I tell them to make time for meditation, before the children arise or after they go to sleep."

"As you begin to find more time for God, you will find less need for sleep, as refreshment is found in meditation. Rising up, even in the middle of the night, for meditation will refresh you, and you will be able to fall back asleep quicker for additional rest. This does not mean that you should set an alarm clock for the middle of the night. It simply means that, if you can't get to sleep upon going to bed or you awaken during the night and can't sleep, meditate for a while. Soon you will realize you will be able to fall back asleep more quickly, and the quality of sleep will refresh you, no matter the length of sleep-time."

"I also advise them, 'During the day, tell the children you need quiet time to talk things over with God. Set an example and invite the children to meditate with you. Help them set up their own quiet place with you, or away from you, or even outside. Children understand more about God than we give them credit for.'"

"Ah . . . Saint Ta, it is beautiful to hear children pray. Children want to know about God."

"That reminds me of a young grandson who visited us last summer. He is very active and does not settle down easily. My husband, daughter, grandson and I were about to enter the building for the Sunday service, when I decided it would be best to hold off going in for as long as possible, so we sat outside. As we were sitting on a bench, he restlessly asked me, 'Why do you have to go to service, Grandma?' I told him, 'I don't have to go to service; I want to go to service.' He asked, 'So, what do you do there?' I replied, 'I learn about God.' He immediately stood up and emphatically said, 'Let's go in now,' so we followed him in. Inside, many were sitting on meditation pillows and others in chairs. He found himself a cushion and followed what others were doing. He was settled, yet curious about all of it."

"Be an instrument, Saint Ta, in helping him and other children know more about God."

I had to stop. I took a deep breath, sighed, and looked out the window. My thoughts were on reaching more children. Jesus had told me to write so that children would understand. I am not so sure the younger ones would, by themselves, but someone could help them.

Recently a granddaughter came to visit us. She is eleven years old and a bright angel. She wanted to read this book. I hesitated, not so sure she would understand it. Then, remembering that Jesus had asked me to write so that children would understand, I reluctantly handed her the first page. She sat down in my big purple chair, snuggled up in it, and started to read. I busied myself with other things, and soon she was right there asking for another page. Again, with some reluctance, I handed her the second page, and again and again she came back asking for more.

I asked her, "Did you understand what you read?" She answered, "I understood enough, Grandma." Once, when she was about seven years old, out of the blue she asked me, "How many lives do we get?" What a profound question from one so young! My response was intuitive and from the heart. I said to her, "I don't know, but I would imagine that it would be up to you." She was satisfied with that.

* * *

"Dear Sweet Jesus, tell me about unconditional love. I realize I can give unconditional love, but even with practice, it seems as if it is not always there. It's a mixed thing. When new people come to me for healing, I can easily give them unconditional love because I don't know them well. But, if I know of someone's bad actions, that makes it harder. And then there is family. I can give them unconditional love because I love every one of them no matter what they have done or do.

"I want to be able to give love unconditionally, all the time to all people, without even having to think about it."

"Unconditional love, Saint Ta, can only be achieved while living in the present moment and not thinking about the past or the future of anyone."

"I would like to think I could give unconditional love to the most wicked."

"Again I repeat, you can if you follow my message to practice living in the present moment and dwell in love."

"It is easier for me to do this, living in our serene surroundings here in the forest. But could I do this if you put me in a situation where my life or a loved one's is threatened by another? Could I give unconditional love then?"

"Blessed are those who are confronted with fear and terror and still dwell in love. They shall have peace."

"What a beautiful, comforting thought. Yet my question might be: When shall we have this peace? Immediately upon confrontations? Or is this a promise for the future?"

"The past is past, and the future is tomorrow, and tomorrow is out of reach. There is only the present, the immediate. As you live each present moment with unconditional love for all of God's creation, in all situations, you become increasingly aware of the presence of God within. In this awareness lies the peace of God, which passeth all understanding. If God is for you, who can be against you?"

"When I work with patients as an occupational therapist or in my healing room, I usually don't know of their past. I give them love from my heart, and I can feel the presence of God. It is easy, like second nature. When a patient or client is having a really bad day, they might direct their frustrations and anger inward or out on me. Instead of feeding into their anger, I visualize You or see the light of God in their faces, Sweet Jesus, and I am reminded that they are individuals and fellow human beings, with feelings of their own, and life is precious. Then the treatments with the patients are ever so much more healing on many levels because they are given with love, and people open up and talk, more readily, about what is bothering them physically, mentally and spiritually. Yes, it is easier to live in love."

"Much help and support are given to those who administer to the sick and needy, from God, masters, angels, and guides. They are ever in God's grace, and there are masters and angels even among them."

"I was working in a hospital in New Mexico, a few years ago. I was asked to do an occupational therapy evaluation on a patient in a four-bed men's ward. I did the evaluation and was about to leave, but the patient was in such misery that I asked him if he would like some 'laying on of hands,' and he said, 'Ah, yes! That would be wonderful.' The other men in the ward were lying very passively, listening, while I worked behind the closed curtain. When I finished, one of the other patients asked, 'Could you possibly do that for me too!?' And I said, 'Sure.' Then one of the patients across the ward said, 'Oh, do me, do me!' So I went over to him too. He appeared to be a rough and tumble type, and I 'did him.' Then he asked, 'How can you do this? How can you do this? You don't even know me!' I said, 'It is called unconditional love,' and he asked, 'You can love even me?' I said, 'Well,

I don't know you. It makes it a lot easier doesn't it?,' and everyone in the ward laughed.

"If you can disregard someone's past—like you said, Jesus, 'Live in the present moment'—then you are able to love unconditionally."

"One has to learn to live in the present moment—the now, the very, very instant you are looking at each other or conversing with each other—and forget all else. That is the now, the present moment. And then it is so much easier to give unconditional love, without regard for the past. If you know someone has done wrong, you are thinking in the past. If you only look at people in the present moment—in their sorrow, their anger, their fear—just look at them in that very present moment and forget the rest— unconditional love comes very easily.

"To forgive is divine. When you unconditionally love another, you have forgiven them, and, in this action, you rid yourself of all the hatred and bitterness, which twists your soul and makes you sick of body, heart, mind, and spirit. I tell you, do not hesitate to forgive."

"I wish I could say that I am perfect in my love for all. I have such wonderful revelations given to me and wonderful experiences, and yet I still get upset, angry, and don't always control my emotions well. Is it possible to be perfect?"

"It is difficult for most people to recognize perfection within their imperfections. Can you get past your perceived imperfections and let go of them and go on? You are perfect."

"I can try.

JUST AS YOU ARE

Facing the fiery setting sun,
I stood upon the river mirror. . . .
"Walk with me." said my God,
as He came ever nearer.

I fell upon the four of me
and hung my head and cried.
"Courage child and come with me."
Then He wiped clear my eyes.

I rose with help to humbly say,
"Just as I am?". . . He nods.
I walked with Him along the way,
Just me, my soul and God.

He showed me branches of the forks
upon the river's life,
it's dangers, beauty, turbulence
with Him by my side.

We visited some clergy-men,
my ego put aside.
I bravely told them I could heal,
for God was at my side.

"Sounds pretty limp," they said to me,
"pronouncing you can heal.
Be gone and let us have our say,
This is simply too unreal!"

Back on the water, He said to me,
as slowly we did walk,
"Just as you are is fine with Me."
Then we continued with our talk.

"I remember this well, Saint Ta. In loving yourself you will realize you are perfect just the way you are. Remember, love is all there is. In love lies perfection."

"I think that is the title to a song somewhere: 'Love is all there is.'"

"God is love. God is all there is."

"Why doesn't love prevail, if God is love and God is in everything?"

"With the free will of man, the veiled human condition does not allow for love and joy to be fully perceived by all, even when it does exist everywhere and in everyone."

"Ah . . . the veil."

"All are born with a thin veil gently protecting you from the rapture of God. Seeing through the veil, as into a mirror dimly, you see vague memories of God slowly becoming mysteries. Still, you are fully understood by God, and you are never separate from God's love. Even though the veil diffused your memory of knowing God, there was enough remembering so that, as a child, you laughed and cried and played and lived in the present moment. You were able to access your true, creative inner child in loving joy, as your veil was much thinner then.

"For some of you, as you grew older, you conformed into someone others wanted you to be. You became a different person wanting to please everyone and be accepted. In the process, you lost much of your true, joyous, childlike self. You gained fear. For some, there might have been a conflict between whom you projected yourselves as to the

world, and whom you really saw yourself as. Sometimes there was such a big difference that you found it very difficult to adapt.

"To protect your inner child from others, in an attempt to hide under a facade, you added layer upon layer of veil, and, in the process, enmeshed into the veil all your perceived fears and anger. And your awareness of God's love dimmed even more.

"You are still hiding under that veil. Your own true self, as spirit and as an inner child full of love and joy, is still very much alive underneath the veil."

This reminded me of a vision I had recorded from long ago. I want to share it here.

THE VEIL

Within the confines of our veil,
there is a sense of belonging
upon the earth plane.
Just as a bride's shyness is covered
with fine netting,
there is a false sense of safety.

I am intrigued by the other side,
yet I hold back, unsure.
If I remove this veil, what is there?
What do I lose? What do I gain?

I wish there was a crack to see through,
with a clear picture of
what I might be getting myself into.
There is no crack,
only this shield of concealing veil.

Can I return if I lift the veil and leave?
Can I simply peek?
If there is bliss,
will all that bliss be boring
after an aeon or two?
Can I give of myself over there?
Will I lose myself?

The jump is so frightening
that I shall just close my eyes and leap.
To land where?
To soar into nothingness?

Will I go to God?
Can I return?
Will I be free?
Will I be happy?
What are my options?

"Once you learn to realize and find comfort in God, your fears slowly subside. As you learn to forgive self and others, and love unconditionally, you begin to access your true inner self. You begin to remember your truth as love and joy. Increasingly, you grow in spiritual awareness of the unity of all, and the veil becomes thinner and thinner and your creativity begins to reawaken within you and your

world is brighter. New revelations are opened up to you, leading you to ever-more spiritual experiences for the growth of the soul. Finally, after peeling off layers of the veil, you will find you, the loving, joyful, creative inner child. For as such is the kingdom of God.

"*Most people are not ready to eliminate the veil all at once. Even you, yourself, said in prose you wrote some time ago:*

> *'She lifts the veil slowly . . .*
> *long enough for a glimpse.*
> *That's all I want to see,*
> *for now.'*"

"Ah yes, I remember well."

Leaving Jesus, I began to relive the incident that prompted that prose.

One night, shortly after my awakening, I suddenly was confronted with all the events in my life that had caused me to be someone other than my spirited, creative self. Terror-filled memories from my past, seemingly all out of proportion, began building, one upon another, in a nightmare. Within a crescendo of chaotic, deafening noise, I was shown all my fears and realized I was living a fear-based life in a fear-based society. I had been afraid of not being good enough, unworthiness, abandonment, not fitting in, not being able to support my family, abuse, loneliness, sickness, accidents, death. And, in those life-long fears, I became a master of being what I thought others wanted me to be. All of these underlying fears had been building up within me for years, and I didn't realize it until they all came to the surface at once.

I was abruptly thrown awake in the midst of the ear-splitting terror, screaming and in a cold sweat. The child within me came to me as separate, and yet, as my own self. I recognized her as myself and she recognized me as herself. We clung together in bed, crying aloud, comforting each other, this child and I. I realized then who I had been and what I had lost, and the constant struggle I had been going through to retain my original self. I knew I had to set aside all the fears that had made me who I was.

Now the child within was showing me how to be me once again, helping me realize that, because they were "my" fears, it was indeed I who had caused my true self to be hidden under a thick veil. I realized there is no justifiable bitterness, and that blaming others had kept me away from unconditional love for all people and situations. It was no one else's fault.

The awakening had prepared the way for this nightmare to happen, which in turn, opened me to even more of my true creative nature, and my veil became thinner and thinner. After the awakening, and especially after this nightmare, I wrote many poems and prose.

THE CHILD WITHIN

"I am the child."
For the first time
we embrace. . . .
The child shows me the wounds
that lay hidden for so long.

I comfort the child. . . .
The child teaches me
what I'd let slip by.
It was in the mists,
veiled like gossamer,
blurred and distorted.
She lifts the veil slowly . . .
long enough for a glimpse.
That's all I want to see,
for now.
A small bit is healed.
"I will never leave you,"
she says.
I hold the child
to gain comfort, and
find the child crying.
I am the child.
I am the adult.
"I will never leave you,"
I say.

After typing this to share with all of you, Jesus, ever-present, said, *"You must all learn to love self and others as an innocent child would. You all have that child within. Let the past go. Let your fears go. Forgive yourself. Forgive everyone. Live in the present moment as the child you are, and love yourself and all others unconditionally. Remember the saying, 'live, love and be happy.' Practice all of these things until they become second nature to you, and you will begin to lift layers of veil from yourself, more and more, bringing you closer and closer to God.*

"With fear, you create ever-deeper layers of veil to protect your inner emotion and creativity. Thus fear keeps you from discovering God. It is only through fearless practice of forgiveness, love and meditation, as a little child, that you can get above the condition of the world you have all created and become closer to God, for to such belongs the kingdom of heaven.

"Saint Ta, imagine: if all people were living in the now with forgiveness and love, all veils would be lifted. There would be nothing to fear. Then you would have realized heaven on earth. Humanity is only beginning to understand the mysteries of Self and God."

"I am humbled by Your presence and guidance in my life, Sweet Jesus. May the words of my mouth and the meditations of my heart be acceptable to You."

I have often come to a standstill between revelations, thinking that finally I had received all that was coming to me and that there couldn't possibly be more. Now, Jesus telling us that humanity is just beginning makes it plain that there will be ever-new revelations as a part of our ongoing spiritual growth.

It was my awakening that triggered access to my inner child and, hence, increased the creativity within me, which, further, made way for me to connect with the spirit world. With the awakening and the lifting of the veil, my mind opened up to seeing ever-more beautiful images of creation. Fear does not exist there in the blissful awareness of beauty; just pure, unconditional love.

* * *

"Sweet Jesus, are all people capable of loving?"

"Yes, but to love unconditionally, that is the answer."

"You mean . . . 'That is the question.' Are all people capable of unconditional love?"

"No, I mean, 'That is the answer.' All people are capable of unconditional love. To live in the present moment and to love unconditionally is what people have to work on . . . all people. Do the best you can and then some, and whatever you do, do it with love and in the present moment."

"Sweet Jesus, I have been thinking about how important it is to be able to receive love. I feel that, in order to be able to give unconditional love, one must first be able to be comfortable with and feel worthy of receiving love."

I almost didn't get the words out, when Jesus rushed in with His message, as if He wanted to share a wonderful revelation:

"Why limit yourselves so? Forget the past. Let go and open your heart to receive love from God and others. God loves you . . . yes, even you! When you can believe that God loves you and you can allow that love to expand within your heart, this acceptance will make it easier for you to give love because you will see and feel all things with love. When you accept and are filled with God's love, your love will begin to overflow in abundant joy. People you know will be aware of the over-abundant love you have to give and they, too, will change toward you. Don't limit your-

selves to just giving love. In receiving love, you will learn how to love yourself more and more. In receiving love, you will increasingly learn to give love to others and, in that giving, you will increasingly learn to accept even more love from others, yourself, and God."

"So many people feel unworthy or even worthless."

Jesus didn't give me time to say more. He was adamant in his response. *"Worthless deems you as meaningless and without significance. God did not create anything insignificant. Worthy deems you as deserving. God never said He loves one person more than another, no matter who they are. Look at the contrast between Old Testament history, that often speaks of unworthiness, to the New Testament, in which I only once spoke the word 'unworthiness.' I came with a new covenant that speaks of love.*

"So many religious organizations have been assertive in deeming mankind as unworthy or undeserving of God's love. Woe to those who take it upon themselves to judge, for even religious organizations reap what they sow. Rules, judgments, and traditions that speak of unworthiness have been wrought out of human arrogance. They should help and teach their people to do what is right and loving, without condemnation, by setting loving examples.

"God's commandments were not ultimatums to make anyone feel guilty but to teach them how to start over, day by day if needed, to learn of and live in love.

"Shake the dogmatic concept of being unworthy. You are a child of God. God loves you no matter what you do. Everything you do is valuable in your spiritual growth,

whether you deem it wrong or right. You learn from mistakes, even the serious ones, and you learn from giving and receiving love. It is never too late."

A friend of ours knew a psychologist who had a practice near a great church. He asked the psychologist if he had any of the parishioners for clients. "Many," he said, and, when asked what the most prominent problem was, he replied, "Guilt."

"Is it easier to receive love if we love ourselves more?"

"You must ask the question, 'Why can't I love myself more?' Love of self is as important as loving your neighbor or even God. There is nothing wrong with loving oneself. Forgive yourself so that, in turn, you can love yourself and others. Look within to find the love within. You do know how to love. You were born loving. If there is love within you for anything under the sun, then you can love yourself for loving that 'anything under the sun.'

"You are capable of loving yourself. If you can imagine that God loves you, no matter what you have done or have become, then you can begin to realize your worthiness and begin to love yourself more. There is nothing that you have done that is unforgivable. God loves you.

"I implore you . . . stop what you are doing. . . . Right now, stop . . . take a deep breath and hold it a second. . . . Now sigh it out. . . . Do it again . . . deep breath, hold, sigh . . . clear your mind. . . . Do this until you feel more relaxed. Now with each breath and hold, as you sigh out . . . say your name. . . . Breathe, hold, sigh, say your name . . . over and over. Think warm thoughts of yourself. . . . Say

*your name again and again until you can smile. . . . You
will begin to find love within.*

*"If this exercise causes you to cry, then cry and start
over, and then over again. You are simply releasing self-
destructive, non-loving thoughts. Dwell on what you know
is good about yourself. Grow on those thoughts. You are
worthy of self-love, self-respect and self-esteem. Love yourself as I love you."*

There was a time in my life when I had great difficulty
saying my name. I was in a relationship in which I was
made to feel near worthless. Over and over I was told how
useless I was, resulting in my lack of self-esteem and self-
love. When someone asked my name, I would slur it all together so that it didn't even sound like my name. It was the
grace of God that guided me through and out of that tragic
situation.

"Sweet Jesus, how can we be sure another person's love
is genuine?"

*"To all I say, if you are experiencing what someone tells
you is love, and it doesn't feel pure and sweet, then it is not
love. If you are experiencing demands on your love by another, then it is not love. Say out loud to that person, 'I
don't deserve how you treat me,' and mean it . . . believe it.
If you remain in an abusive relationship, you may be punishing yourself. If you continue to accept negative treatment, you may simply be accepting it because you think you
deserve it. It may be a subconscious need.*

*"You may feel that there is no way out of your unloving
relationship. Do not hesitate to seek financial, medical,*

psychological, protective, or spiritual help when you need it to free yourself from an unloving relationship. God does not want you in any abusive relationship; however, you may be able to change the relationship for the better through counseling and guidance. If not, move on with your life.

"Learn from your lessons. Even unloving relationships hold lessons. Recognizing the relationship as a lesson may be the first step toward learning the lesson. The lesson may be in strengthening your ability to give love to the unloving.

"Have you been honest and up-front with the other person? Honesty is never wrong. Does the other person simply want out of the relationship? Are your needs so strong that you are hanging on, disregarding the feelings of another? Is your love for that person keeping you from moving on with your life? If so, lovingly forgive, let go and move on. Do not dwell on unhappiness. It is beneath you. You do not deserve unhappiness. Start fresh. Find comfort in God, and new doors will be opened for you.

"Love is polite and caring. Love is honoring and giving. Love is kind and accepting of others' faults. Love is patient, undemanding, honest and forgiving. Love is being able to let go. By knowing all of this and using your intuition to trust and take chances, you will be able to determine if your love or another person's love is genuine."

"That's two different things, trust and taking chances."

"Trust in your intuition. It will be immediate. If you think too long, doubt can stand in the way of true intuition and can confuse you. True intuition would tell you, imme-

diately, whether a person has genuine love for you or not. If hesitation stands in the way, then you have to determine if what you are listening to is really intuition or doubt. It would be best not to determine a person's genuine love on one incident, using intuition, where there is doubt. If you have difficulty trusting in other situations, then you may not be open to listening to your intuition. In that case, it is more likely doubt that you are dealing with, and you will not be able to trust as readily.

"Some people are very afraid of taking chances. But not you, Saint Ta. It has been said before that you have plowed through lives with a purposeful attitude, like a cow catcher on the front of a train! You have heeded the calling of Spirit, listened, and sailed through, trusting God would guide you."

"My mother often said to me, 'How can you be taking such chances? What if you fail?' My answer was, 'Well, then I can pick myself up, brush myself off, and start all over again.' I learned many lessons, some harder than others. They allowed for growth. I view the lessons and the learning along the way as an important part of my life."

"Trusting and taking chances are an important part of the journey."

"So, taking a chance to trust someone's love when it feels intuitively right is an important step in learning to receive love."

"Yes."

"Sometimes people get hurt after trusting someone. It

sets them back. And this happens on the job or with friends, not just with someone they love."

"*That is true. Some people don't know how to use their intuition to recognize truth in any situation. They mix up the signals that come from others.*

"*Some people get sex and love mixed up. The feelings sex gives seem so blissful and yet are not always so. Sex is not love.*"

"Are you saying that sex is to be avoided?"

"*Not at all. There is no shame in loving, genuine and pure sex. When two people lovingly open the whole self to give to each other, then sex is good. When sex is carnal and not from the heart, then it is not loving. It must be from the whole person, with loving respect and pure intention. Then you will experience loving sex as none other. I repeat, if you are experiencing what someone tells you is love and it doesn't feel pure and sweet, then it is not pure love. If you are experiencing demands on your love by another, then it is not pure love. If the love you are giving is to fulfill your needs and not the other person's and is selfish, then it is not pure love. Love is polite and caring. Love is honoring, sharing and giving. Love is kind and accepting of others' faults. Love is patient, undemanding and forgiving.*

"*Youth must be especially careful. The freshness of youth may give one the delusion that sex is love. It is not. Sex is a physical act. You can have love without sex. But, you should not have sex without true love. In this physical act you might receive what you perceive as love because of your own selfish desires. In your desire to experience sex, you will not find love, you will only fulfill desire. You might think you want to please another by offering sex, because you feel sorry for him or her, or you might want to win them over. Someone may badger you long enough for you to give in. You might feel down about something and seek sex for comfort. You might feel that everyone is doing it, so it is okay. You might think getting high on sex or drugs is bliss.*

"You are more intelligent than these deceiving notions. There is no love in these situations. If you have had these feelings, now is the time to change and stop what you are doing to yourself and others.

"You can be comfortable and happy on your own. Learning to live within one's self is a good place to be for spiritual growth. When you are happy, others will feel that happiness and may want to share it with you.

"Getting high on God is the ultimate, loving bliss—and not the kind of bliss perceived by some humans as experienced through drugs and carnal sex. That is not bliss. That is messing with the physical pleasure centers of the body and mind, not of the spirit. And it is too demanding on your soul.

"There remains a risk of sexually-transmitted diseases, more now than there ever was. Precaution or abstinence is necessary. You have the world at your fingertips: computers, libraries, books and governmental resources that inform people. Check it all out. Read and make yourself aware. Do not be shy or embarrassed about it. Now is the time to take responsibility for the rest of your life and the lives you may create. There can only be respect for your concerns.

"*Women, listen carefully. You are the image of the Divine Mother, who gives birth to creation. It is an honor bestowed upon you that your body has the possibility to lovingly create, nourish and care for a child of God, both before and after birth. You must cherish this honor by making right choices out of love. Recognize and honor the divinity in the father of your children.*

"*Honor is bestowed upon you, also, for the love and care you give all Mother Earth's inhabitants. And you are capable of being self-sustaining in the physical world around you.*

"*Men, listen carefully. You are the image of the Divine Father, who is beyond creation. This means you are more than creation. Yes, you can co-create a child, but you must be even more than that. You must show great strength through your right choices before and after conception. You must share in providing love, shelter and sustenance for your family and raising your children. Recognize and honor the divinity in the mother of your children.*

"*Women have been mistreated as less than man far too long. There is no honor in treating women in any way but with love and respect. Woe to the man or woman who does not see their mate as equal. Remember one is no better than another in the eyes of God.*

"*To those who cannot have children: There are many children who do not have parents, who are desperate for love and homes. Adopting and fostering a child is a reciprocal blessing. For those of you who do not want or cannot have children of your own: There are many situations where you can care for children during the day and be in your own home at night. There are many ways you can help children: in the medical field, activities, babysitting, spiritual growth, and by setting a good example.*

"It is disheartening to observe so many single mothers and absent fathers, and single fathers and absent mothers. Most often these single parents start out quite young. Your societies do not always provide the young the opportunity to share parenthood with respect in their dire circumstances.

"There will be more and more need for extended families to live together as time goes on. It will be the way of the future. Grandparents are already taking more responsibility for the young. Grandparents have lived longer and have learned more about life through experience and can teach the young right living and right thinking. Youth, in turn, can teach the grandparents what they have learned. Unconditionally taking care of the children so that young parents can grow in responsibility is an act of love. On the other hand, the young should realize the tremendous responsibility they are placing on grandparents and take that responsibility upon themselves when possible.

"It has been said, 'It takes a whole village to raise a child.' That is truth. Already communities are forming to share in the responsibility of raising children and to support one another. This is a wonderful concept. However, be aware, and do this on a trial basis for a short time, until you are sure you want to live in a specific community. Talk to people who live there and who have left there. Do not expect this situation to be a place to be lazy. The best ones are a balance of love, worship, work and play. There are

good communities, and there are extremist communities that make demands that are against loving principles."

I stopped here to contemplate on all of this. I was filled with information that may not have been new to me, and yet, all of this was summarized so concisely and to the point that I had to think on it. It was like I was hearing it for the first time.

And then, almost in the next breath, without thinking about it, I asked, "What is 'tough love'?"

"Tough love goes along with unconditional love. It is not easy to provide tough love. It may appear to the giver and the recipient that there is no love at all. With tough love, you withhold help that someone might have been depending on to the point of relying on it too much. There are many situations that call for tough love. The person might be lazy. They might not be working or looking for work. They might not be going to school. They might be on drugs or other substance abuse. They might be taking advantage of you in many ways. Tough love often makes things worse before the situations get better. In time, tough love allows the person to grow and gives the person self-esteem and the realization that they are capable of doing things on their own. It takes strength, time, and love to be able to do this successfully. It should not be interpreted as non-loving. There should be no guilt. Tough love is one of the greatest forms of love to give. It is unconditional love at its best."

"Sweet Jesus, I feel such love for those people that have to go through this.

"I wrote a poem some time ago about unconditional

love. Would you like to hear it?"

"Your poetry has a language all its own. I would love to hear it."

"I'll bet you already know it."

"Don't you like to listen to the same music over and over?"

"Yes."

"And I would like to hear your poem again."

OH . . . MY FRIEND

Here might I stay a while . . .
and ponder of the oceans . . .
of the sky . . . so nigh
and yet so far from I.

Here might I play . . .
upon the winds of time. . .
and depth of life . . .
and sing a while of love.

Here might I gladly spend
all my days
with grief of thine . . .
to soothe you and relieve you . . . friend.

Here might I think a while . . .
not too long or chance goes by,
to give myself for you . . .
as I am you and you are love.

Here might I listen . . .
for the tears and quiet thoughts
and words unspoken and pain untold . . .
to send the loveless love . . .
and see a life unfold.

Here might I give you love . . .
and in that love, Oh . . . my friend . . .
you might know that from whence we came
is where we are and are going . . .
All is joyful love the same.

"Saint Ta, I love this poem. Love is universal. When I say that, I don't say it lightly. Love is the fuel that keeps the universes going. Love lives within you and keeps you going. It is life force. Love cancels fear. Love cannot be subjected to labels. Love has no opposites. It stands alone. It is pure and sweet."

I felt overwhelming love given to me by Jesus. I was stilled. No words were necessary. There are no words in our vocabulary to explain love such as this. There is no greater love.

I had to stop here. I was suddenly overcome by an all-pervading fragrance of roses. My body closed in upon itself. I cannot explain the immensity of the energy within. There are no words. The fragrances and bliss just come, sometimes for no apparent reason. I can only wait until after the fragrances pass before I can write of them. "Thank you, Sweet Jesus . . . for your loving presence in my life. I love you."

Chapter Four

Mother Earth ~ Mother Nature

It would seem impossible that anyone,
however incrusted with care,
could escape the Godful influence of these
sacred fern forests.

—John Muir

Deep in the forest at Song of the Morning, where the ferns carpeted the forest floor and the birds and the wind in the trees greeted me, I took off my shoes to walk on the beautiful, moss-covered, mile-long path that led to the Christ Shrine. There, George was waiting for me, for us to be married. We wore rose garlands and spring colors, and the sun was bright and the sky was blue. Here, within this lovely emerald cathedral, a guitarist played music and sang with the forest dwellers. In a ceremony, using our words and the words of others, we were married by a dear friend, in the company of family, friends and others who just happened by.

During the Sunday service that followed, I sang a love song to my husband, accompanied by the guitarist. Friends made a special Sunday dinner at the Retreat, with a wedding cake and sparkling juice. It was truly a blessed, beautiful spring day, full of enchantment, in the year two thousand.

And once again, spring is here. The calendar says it is; however, in this part of Michigan, warm weather usually lags behind. There is a feeling of expectancy and freshness within the forest. It is always a miracle to me how Mother Nature gifts us each spring with an emergence of primroses, daffodils, tulips, hyacinths and fiddle-head ferns, all emerging from under a thin blanket of snow.

I have often contemplated how Mother Nature is different from Mother Earth. To me, Mother Nature envelopes the whole of creation, including universes. Mother Nature is God in nature. Within Her realm is Mother Earth, who ensouls the earth and its atmosphere. Mother Earth is a part of Mother Nature. Within her own evolution, Mother Earth reveals God's presence through beauty and intelligent power, and provides an environment in which humans and other life forms can live and interact and express divinity. Both Mother Nature and Mother Earth are the physical part of creation, as well as the spirit that envelopes and permeates it.

God is sometimes worshipped as a universal Divine Mother, who creates and lovingly sustains all of nature. The masters tell us that God is both within and beyond creation, within the world of time and space as well as beyond it.

I address Jesus, ever present, "Sweet Jesus, when I became aware of my healing gift several years ago, I was so engrossed in the human condition that I often overlooked the marvelous world of Mother Nature and its correlation to the Omnipresent God. Oddly enough, it took a simple little critter to remind me."

"The children would especially enjoy your stories of nature. It was such fun watching you open to the realizations set before you."

"You were aware of my experiences?"

"Ah yes. Your rememberings shone brighter than lamp light. You couldn't be missed."

"Pretty funny!"

"I am being serious. You shine. Everyone shines their light, some brighter than others. How do you think it is that you can send others light if you didn't have it inside of yourself?"

"I never thought of that. People often ask me how to shine light on others. It is difficult to explain."

"One simple way to explain it would be to tell people to smile on self and others."

"Wow, what a pleasant thought." I hesitated, smiling to myself, before going on. "Sitting here, smiling, I can't help but think loving, happy thoughts."

"Yes, and you are shining brighter because of it. Now let's hear the critter story."

Instead, I sat and smiled for a good long moment before

continuing. I remembered people in hospitals and nursing homes, aged and children. I remembered how they seemed to "light up" when they were smiled at.

Jesus interrupted my thoughts, *"Smiling brings happy thoughts."*

Laughing, I said to Jesus, "Good things do come in small packages. I became more aware of the wonders of Mother Nature from some little critters. I was ready, then, to move on into realizations about all living things.

"Before I moved to the Retreat, I lived alone in my home on the banks of the Manistee River. Even then, I spent time meditating and quieting myself in the evenings after work or the early morning hours before work. One day, as I was bathing, I noticed something in the bath water. It looked like very-heavy, straw-like hair. I took it out and laid it on the edge of the bathtub and looked at it closely. I was moved to blow on it. Nothing moved. I couldn't recognize it as anything but debris. I left it there and went off to work.

"When I came home from work and went into the bathroom, there in its place stood the most magnificent daddy-long-legs spider imaginable. At that time, I had a healthy fear of spiders. I would shriek like the best of us at even the tiniest spider. But this spider was special. He stood tall and proud. I recognized him as the debris I had left behind.

"I said to the spider, 'I am going to save your life for the second time today.' I got a clear cup and a sheet of paper from the kitchen. I returned to the bathroom, placed the cup over the spider, and as I slowly pushed the paper under it, he crawled onto the paper. I now had captured a spider. I looked him over closely through the clear cup and marveled at him. He wasn't afraid. Nor was I. He stood within the cup, tall and healthy. I took him outside and, as I released him, I wished him well.

"From that moment in time, I became more connected to and conscious of the insect and critter world. I came to the conclusion that I could no longer kill anything thoughtlessly. Now I always do my best to communicate with all of nature's critters. There have been very few times that I felt I had to kill them. But, when I did, it was without malice.

"Spring arrived, one year, with the usual infestation of ants, and I wondered what to do about them. A friend told me to talk to them. So I sat myself down on the floor and talked to the line of ants. Using heart talk, I said to them, 'I am honored by your visit, but this is my home and you have the great outdoors. I ask that you honor my home by leaving, and I will try my best to honor your outdoor home.' Nothing happened. I still had the ants. I went back to my friend and told her it didn't work, and she said, 'You have to talk to the queen ant.' Well, I didn't know there was such a thing as a queen ant. But I thought I'd give it a try anyway. So, once again, in the midst of a line of marching ants, I sat to talk to the queen ant. With a feeling of great respect, I told her, 'I am honored by your presence, oh great queen ant. I would ask that you honor my home by redirecting your ants to the great outdoors. It would be much safer for your ants to be outside, and I will honor their home outside.' Guess what? No more ants! I was amazed. I never thought it would happen, and yet I let myself believe that it was possible, and it was. I felt really good about talking with the ants. I didn't have to kill them. As time has gone on, I have felt more and more connected to the insect world. I am always looking forward to my next encounter.

"Heart talk is how I talk to God and masters, and now the animals, plants, insects, and more. It is a loving, feeling process, using the heart and mind, and sometimes voice, to communicate. It is holding a conversation in your own language, often without mouthing the words. It may seem one-sided, and yet I feel acknowledged by the insect or animal or plant. Heart talk seems to be universal. It is as if we all speak the same language and there really is no language barrier. As if we are all one. And we are."

"Saint Ta, your heart talk is magnetically connecting you to the consciousness of nature's inhabitants, through your love. You are right, love is the language that all of creation understands. Nature is always ready to communicate; it is the human that needs to open up. Nature is attracted to your consciousness when you, in turn, acknowledge nature and all of creation with love.

"Intermingling of your consciousness and nature's consciousness requires communication. In this lifetime, most humans have forgotten the language of nature. If you want to be able to connect with nature you must respectfully begin by simply talking to nature in any language, with love. All creation has consciousness and language. Even the trees communicate with the birds that nest within their branches. Even mothers and fathers communicate back and forth with their babies, with love, before the babies are

born and able to verbally speak. Connection to Mother Nature requires that you learn to communicate through heartfelt love.

"When you reach out to nature through loving thoughts and feelings, nature will acknowledge you through your senses. You can experience nature's loving response in many different ways: through vision, fragrances, feelings, hearing, tasting, or through just knowing, as in intuition.

"Mankind is too wrapped up in just words. They have lost the creative side of communication."

"I once heard a recording made of the sound of crickets slowed according to the ratio between a cricket's and a human's life-span. The sound was that of a heavenly chorus, harmonious and beautiful."

"All of nature dwells in harmony and love. It is only man that has to learn of this."

"Someone recently asked me, 'What about the lion tearing into the flesh of its prey, or hundreds of acres of forest killed by an infestation of bugs?' He was saying, 'How could this be if nature dwells in love?'"

"Ah, your dear friend has such a beautiful bond with nature. And yet, in his musings, he must become more mindful of the harmonious plight of all of nature on this wheel of life, death, life . . . daytime, night-time, daytime . . . good days, followed by bad days, followed by good days. It may appear discordant to you. Yet, life on earth is harmoniously cyclical and, within these cycles, comes new life into life, all dwelling in the love of God, which permeates

all of nature. Mother Earth cleanses herself, and then allows destructive forces to build up, then recleanses herself, daily or even millennium to millennium. Time is meaningless because of its harmonious nature. Everything repeats over and over, in different human-perceived time frames, as the wheel keeps turning.

"In order to get off the wheel, you must become nonattached to the cycles, let go and let God. At the same time, live your life in the presence of God while caring for and giving to nature and others. Become more and more mindful of God's love in all things. Look deep into the eyes of the lion and you will find God. Look deep into the destructive insects and you will find God. Within God's oneness are earth and all of its inhabitants, dwelling in love, often unaware."

"I once wrote a short poem while in a feeling of oneness with Mother Earth. It speaks of remembering the oneness."

MEMORIES

Upon my waking meditation,
a vision flashed . . .
of memories, forever young
and eons repeated, repeated. . . .
Dullness gone of inbetweens,
my visions deeply seated.

As orchestrated breath, I sing. . . .
Within the words, the sounds do ring.
My vapor . . . luminescent whim . . .
ribbon like and freely swims
within the earthbound atmosphere.
I am LOVE. . . . I AM here.

"Food for thought, Saint Ta. Why aren't you writing more poetry? Poetry is language generated by consciousness of the One. Whether the poem is of love or war, it is still generated through the remembrance of the One. A creative connection from the heart and soul."

"This book has me so wrapped up in meditating and writing that I haven't given poetry much thought."

"Do not allow writing books to take away from your SELF. Your singing and poetry are outlets for you. Your poetry expresses very deep-seated thoughts, experiences and feelings other people need to hear. And you connect with The Divine through your singing. Do not neglect yourself to write this book or any book."

I stopped momentarily and looked up and out the windows. The sun was shining its warm glow onto the lush forest and into our living room. I felt happiness flow through me, and all of nature seemed to be smiling with me.

"Thank you, Sweet Jesus.

"Sweet Jesus, living under a canopy of forest, we realize the wisdom the trees impart in their beautiful patience. They seem more resigned to the way they have to live than even I. I often tell people to sit at the base of a tree and put their back up to the tree, or stand and hug the tree and get comfortable; then communicate with the tree, sharing thoughts and troubles, and then listen. Many, many people come to me and tell me how meaningful their experience was.

"Saint Ta, you and George live your innate connection to nature. It is easy for you to do, since you live in nature. It is extremely hard for those people who live in a sea of asphalt, cement and steel, and find entertainment night after night in a box to realize nature around them. People feel they are in a world lacking opportunities to connect with nature. You and George have found the natural relationship with nature that all mankind is capable of and has within.

"Nature is there for all people—young, old and all races—and will speak to their heart if they would just take the time to become aware of the love-generated life force which is in all consciousness. All of your material goods are provided by Mother Earth. Nature is never absent from you. Nature is not separate from you. It is universal and The Divine in nature is universal."

"I feel that, if you can quiet yourself to commune with nature, you are communicating with God—whether it is a tree or a flower."

"There is divinity in nature."

"How can we know the divinity in nature?"

"When you are aware of the oneness of all there is, you

will realize that nature is also of God. People have forgotten how to be aware of the divine connectedness of nature to self. The divinity in nature and humans is evident when you realize that all is one in God."

"How can others learn to connect with nature?"

"You are living what others should be doing, even on a limited basis. Song of the Morning affords you constant retreat. Yet I say to you, there are innumerable areas where one can find God in nature. Nature is found everywhere you turn, including right out the back door, or the city park, or the flowers and produce at the corner grocery store, or the rising or setting sun. Surround yourself with nature when you can. Go on yearly retreats, away from your busy lives, to find and quiet yourself and thus connect with nature. Children should be encouraged to connect with nature in quiet settings, too."

"Children are more attuned to nature than we give them credit for. Years back, in the autumn, as my daughter and her very young son were riding in a car, he started crying. It was not like him to cry in such a loud, lamenting manner. When his mother asked what the matter was, he sadly cried out, 'All the leaves are falling off the trees!'"

This reminded me of a day when George and I were sitting outside in the rose garden at Song of the Morning, listening to nature in the rustling leaves and feeling the sun, warm on our faces.

NATURE'S SYMPHONY

As we rested within the rose garden,
on a most beautiful, warm evening,
the sky displayed its glories and
nature played its symphony.

Listening, in the stillness of the night,
inside our awareness,
the evening responded to the
quietude of our nature.

The trees clapped and the wind whistled
and the birds sang,
as we softly breathed
the fragrances of lilting melodies.

As each sound emerged,
our silence grew louder,
our hearts inarticulate
before us.

I held my breath,
as if breath was unimportant.
I closed my thoughts,
waiting for you to open them.

God was there then
in the sheer silence
of the space between us. . . .

No matter the symphony cannot be repeated. . . .
It will come again as another song
to refresh our spirits
when we sit to rest.

"It is doubly-important for spiritually-minded people to be connected and grounded to Mother Earth. You cannot progress with your head in the clouds and all things spiritual. You must be balanced with the oneness of reality and spirit to grow. You still have to live in your environment and support yourselves. Actions are as important as meditation."

"Some of the people who come to the retreat to live and work are very spiritually oriented. They want to hide from the world so that they can spend their time in meditation. They want to live in the world but not of it. I have to continually tell them to connect with nature, to keep grounded. When they are not grounded, their auric field is imbalanced.

"Even so, there are some, like you and George, who are so attuned to the harmony of nature and God that they live in the constant oneness, walking and working in the presence of God. They have found what they have been searching for. They are rarely found living in retreats. They tend to isolate themselves, and do not have ego, and do not make noisy shows of their meditations or progress."

"Am I too noisy about my meditations and progress?"

"Even if the sharing seems to be concentrated on you, it is not about you. Disown it. Your sharing is about what these writings will do for others."

"Jesus, I am always filled with never-ending joy in the new revelations given to me. Thank you for all that you are sharing."

"There are no limits to spiritual remember-ing/revelations. They will come to those of you who are open. Many of you feel spiritual growth has to be difficult and big. Think easy and small steps. Spiritual revelations and growth can come even in seemingly unimportant events in your lives in the form of lessons. There is no limit to God."

"I learned a wonderful lesson from a dog some time ago. I was working in New Mexico and my assistant occupational therapist and friend told me her dog was to have surgery soon, and she wondered if it would be all right if she brought the dog into the rehabilitation area, in a cage, during recovery. Well, the day arrived and so did she and the dog. First she carried in a large cage and then she went out to carry in the dog. He was quite a big dog and was heavy for her to carry and put in the cage. He was still under the effects of the anesthesia. We went about our work and, when things slowed down, I said to her, 'How would you like me to do energy work on your dog?'

"The words just spilled out of my mouth. I had never worked with animals before and wasn't even sure if they had auras! She opened the cage and pulled the dog out. The dog was so out of it from the anesthesia that he did not make any signs of awareness. I proceeded to say a prayer and then, very slowly, I scanned for his aura. Immediately, I felt it and then smoothed his aura out! She rolled him over and, again, I slowly smoothed out his aura on the other side. I also worked on healing the incision. After we were finished, she put him back in the cage.

"A few weeks later, we had a terrible ice storm. I was

afraid to venture out to go home after work. My friend offered to let me spend the night in her nearby home, and I was very happy to do so. We arrived at her home and walked in. The dog I had, two weeks earlier, given energy work to was on the other side of the room as we entered. He spied me and ran to me and lay at my feet. Over and over, I slowly smoothed out his aura on one side, and then he rolled over for me to do the other side. It was a joyful, happy reunion. In the morning, as soon as he heard me up, he ran to me and again lay at my feet for more.

"This was a new revelation for me. First of all, that animals have auras. Second, that animals are so remarkable that they can be aware of their surroundings even while anesthetized. Third, that this dog remembered me and my energy. I loved all of it.

"Given that I had chosen not to study or read or listen to anything about healing because I wanted it to come straight from God, I was unaware of the energy of animals. This was a first for me and God provided the lesson through Mother Nature. I was ready for it. All lessons seemed to come when I needed to know something, often through another person, plant, or animal.

"My friend tried to pay me for helping her dog, with money, food and so forth. I realized it was important for her to be able to give me something. I finally accepted a feather, which is still hanging from a planter in my healing room."

"Animals and all forms of nature are sensitive to their surroundings. They are fully aware of the energy of humans. All of nature and even all things have auras, con-

sciousness and life energy."

"Being open to God's guidance, I have grown into a more acute awareness of nature. I feel a connection with an animal when I pet its aura, even though I do not touch it.

"In that very first present moment, when I petted the dog's aura, I came to the realization that everything in creation is made up of energy and has an aura. At that time, I set a prayerful intention for the ability to cleanse all auras—be they of animals, plants, insects, or humans—of the causes of ill health, with God's healing grace. Since then, there is a knowing that the initial intention holds true for all present moments. I do not have to pray or set an intention each time. I just simply know.

"Our cat is about fifteen years old. As soon as I pass my hands over her body, she lies down at my feet. I don't touch her. She stretches out, and rolls over and over as I slowly cleanse her aura. She loves it. She is a feral cat and has long claws. Her claws grab onto the carpet for rolling over but, as she rolls and senses my hands nearby, the claws are instantly retracted. I have learned, from experience, that aura petting reduces pain and heals. I have demonstrated this to many pet owners.

"When I can truly connect with an animal, there is nothing to fear in approaching it. If I sense discomfort from the animal or feel unsure, I back off, just as I would with a human."

"As you radiate love to the animals and become one with them, you know their fears or needs intuitively and are able to respond accordingly. If you become steadfast in the

absence of harmful thoughts toward animals, they will not fear or harm you. It is the law of attraction: what you give you receive."

"Animals don't seem to lack anything from being petted off the body rather than on the body. They always seem very satisfied with hands-off petting. I compare the few that don't like their aura petted with people who don't like you to get close to them. I often find that, if animals don't want their aura petted, they will accept it when you do it further away. Then, most often, they love aura petting as much as the animals that love it closer. More older animals sit still for it than young, very active animals."

"Animals will, most definitely, feel relief or experience healing when you do this for them. Clearing the aura also helps prevent disease from manifesting on the body, even in an animal. Younger animals don't have the patience that the older animals have, so they won't always stand still for it until they need it. They do feel the energy, though, and as you know, are very inquisitive. For them it is often play-time."

"Some time ago, I was visiting a sick friend, who was in a great deal of pain and wanted some healing energy work for himself. We went into his bedroom and he lay down on the bed. One of his two great danes came and stood along-side of me. I had to brace myself because the dog put his body right up against mine and pushed against me. This dog was nearly as tall as I am and he was sitting! The other great dane did not interfere. I started to bring my hands across my friend's body to try to determine where his aura needed work. The dog would push my hands, with his nose, into areas where he thought I should be working. Here was a healer dog!

"When the dog and I finished with the energy work, my friend and I decided to go outside and lie in the sun. We proceeded to lie down on lounge chairs. The two great danes lay down near us. It was a beautiful, sunny day. I noticed many flies in the area and I did some heart talk with them and said, 'I am honored to be in your presence, but I would like to be able to lie in the sun. I would appreciate it if you would let me rest here for a little while, and when I am done, you can have your space back.' . . . No bugs bothered me. After about five more minutes, my friend jumped up and emphatically said, 'I can't stand these flies. I need to get some spray and spray them.' I was very upset, first of all, because I had not spoken for him in the beginning and, second, because he wanted to kill them with spray. He went inside to get the spray. I attempted to talk the flies into leaving. In the meantime, I didn't want to stick around for the kill. So . . . I looked at the great danes, and in silent heart talk, I asked them, 'Would you like to show me your yard and what you do here?' They immediately jumped up and walked off about ten feet, turned around, and looked at me as if to say, 'Well, are you coming or aren't you.' So I got up and followed them. First they took me to one area of the tall stockade fence, which was needed to keep them in the big yard. They barked, and from the other side of the fence another dog barked back. I felt as if I had been introduced to the neighbor dog. Then I followed them down a trail leading through some trees and they showed me where they lie out of the sun. They took me to the fish pond and some other areas also. By then my friend had done his deed, so I thanked the dogs and left them on their own."

"The dogs were blessed to have you in their environment, interacting . . . ."

Interrupting Jesus, I hurriedly said, "Oh, it was a blessing for me to have that experience with the dogs! It was wonderful! I felt honored to be in their world."

"The dogs sensed how you felt when you were able to place yourself within their consciousness for communication. You never considered them at a lower level than you. They were loving that you were willing and able to follow their guidance. They have a high regard for you.

"Living in the oneness and omnipresence of God, with no distinction between yourself and nature, affords you the ability to communicate with the nature world. Animals are very receptive. They have no reason to disbelieve.

"The divine side of universal nature reaches out and melds together all who are in harmony with self, each other and nature. In your reaching out to nature and melding with it, you have created a bond that no one can destroy. You are forever connected, as parent and child, with nature, often reversing roles.

"If all people could feel this bond even where they live, in their own neighborhood or home, they would feel the harmony of all creation. Think a moment . . . if this could be done as a village, town, city, state, or country, the earth environment would be healthier for all humans, and humans would be able to get along with humans.

"Live, love, and teach each other honor and respect for Mother Nature, and Mother Nature will, in turn, teach you many lessons. Mother Nature and you are of the One, not separate."

"One day, I was driving home from a visit with family, through an area where part of the forest was being cleared for a new section of freeway. I came over a hill and saw the clearing. It was as if a giant sickle had been wielded through the forest, taking with it everything in sight—a swath of devastation of the green, for miles. I gasped and had to catch my breath. Immediate sadness came over me. All this for safer travel in this rapidly-growing population, at the expense of Mother Earth."

"Human life is important. It is the growing affluent and materialistic society of today that demands safer travel. If it is done with honor and without malice and intent to harm Mother Earth, it is acceptable. If it is done for excessive monetary profit, it is not acceptable. Mother Earth suffers either way. The devastation to all of nature on and in Mother Earth is evident in war-torn places, forest clearings, diverting of waterways, raping the land of minerals, oil and gas, pollution to the environment and even waste from your households. All of this and more has been as detrimental to Mother Earth and her inhabitants as is the taking of human lives.

"You cannot just take from Mother Earth. You must realize you are taking away from future generations—your children, grandchildren and theirs. If you take a tree, you must plant a tree.

"Be aware of what you are purchasing and throwing away. How much waste are you accountable for? Do you recycle? Do you pollute? Do you have more than you need? You are like the child in the store crying loudly, 'I want . . .' when in fact you do not need.

"I tell you, Mother Earth is more powerful than all your weapons set off at once. Do you not realize that you are working in parallel with Mother Earth. As you advance, so does she. As you become imbalanced, so does she."

"Is this why there is so much drought in some areas and floods in other areas. . . ?"

". . . And seasonal disruptions and melting of polar ice and strange behaviors of animals and people—often caused by man's ignorance.

"Some of the devastation is from Mother Earth's natural cleansing cycles and maintaining equilibrium. And Mother Earth needs more and more cleansing now as human population grows and devastation to humanity and nature increases. Mother Earth does not do harm intentionally. It is in the cleansing process that people get in the way.

"Many humans don't understand that Mother Earth is a part of the whole, just as important as you and I. It is all one."

* * *

"There are so many animal and insect stories I could tell. So much about nature to share, and yet, I have to contain myself. But I would like to share a few plant stories. I think they would help people to see other kinds of experiences that are possible while connecting with nature.

"I once took my mother a beautiful plant for Easter. She enjoys watching them open up from the bud stage, so I always look for plants with a lot of buds. This plant was just budding out. I could imagine how beautiful it was going to be and how she would enjoy its unfolding. Just before I left my mother's apartment to go home, I thought I would give the plant a little energy work to help it on its way to blossoming. The next day, when I talked to my mother, she was upset. The plant had fully blossomed overnight, and the stems could not hold the flowers up and they were strewn over the sides of the table. In its response to the energy, it gave its all.

"Many years ago, we had an ancient peach tree that did not bear fruit. This was before I was aware of energy work. I went up to the tree and asked it to bear fruit for us. The tree bore so much wonderful fruit that year that I was able to can it and make jelly; moreover we enjoyed eating it fresh. I even had peaches enough to share with others.

"We had an unexpected visit, one fine day, from a very-loved brother, Father John. We did not have a lot of money at the time, and yet, I felt I wanted to feed him supper. So, much to my husband's horror, I fixed him leftovers. My husband came from a family that did not make simple meals for guests. I chopped up left-over beef roast and potatoes and made hash. I even placed the bottle of ketchup on the table. It was a simple meal: vegetables and the hash. Then I went outside and picked the fresh peaches. I cut them up and put them in desert dishes with just a little sugar and cream. Father John loved it.

"I sometimes wonder if the peach tree knew of his upcoming visit. I shall never forget that peach tree. It bore fruit when we needed it, and yet, my asking cost the tree plenty. It never bore fruit after that. I realized that I had asked too much of the tree. It often saddens me. Once in a while, nature reminds me to let nature take its course, as in the case of the peach tree and the plant I gave my mother. I am ever so much more careful now."

"The beautiful peach tree and your mother's plant gifted you with a lesson, even as you gifted them with loving energy. You've learned valuable lessons here that speak to all humans. Interfering in nature can bring harm to nature and, in response, harm to humans. There is a domino effect when you mess with nature, not always evident at first.

"Imagine, if you will, that mankind often simply manipulates and eliminates much of nature for their use, pleasure, or just because nature is in the way. The devastating result is detrimental to the future of all mankind.

"Mother Earth is there for you to use in moderation, not to abuse. In all the oneness, nature and God are one. Be extremely conscious when you mess with nature, because you mess with God!"

"I am not too sure I remember this entirely or clearly, but there was a scientist named Bose. He was from India and studied plant life. Bose had an instrument that he called a crescograph. He attached some type of sensor to a leaf of a plant, and when he cut another leaf off that same plant, the crescograph went crazy. It appeared that the plant actually sensed pain from having that leaf cut off. He also attached some sensors to grass and then cut the rest of the grass. The crescograph went crazy. Here was hypothetical evidence of plants having feelings when being cut, and showing signs of caring when nearby plants are cut.

"I remember having dinner with a group of people at the Retreat who were having a casual conversation about why you shouldn't eat four-legged animals. They felt it was inhumane. I told them about Bose and his experiments and asked if maybe we shouldn't be eating fruits and vegetables either, as the plants respond to their demise and even have empathy for other plants too!"

"Plants and animals have lovingly been provided to keep earth in balance and for your use and pleasure. People are unique and from many nationalities, each originally created for and born in their own environment. Now that you can travel from one area to another and live in areas far from your origins, you may not be receiving what you need from your new environment. Seriously think about the food source from the area where you were born and the genealogy of your family. It was the vibration of that area that penetrated into your consciousness. For example, some people cannot tolerate the diet from other cultures in other lands. That is why people are so attracted to their own homelands and often become homesick when away. It is the shared vibration with others within that area that draws them back. The best foods for you are grown in and of the environment of your origin. Those foods may include wildlife, meat, poultry, or fish, along with local fruits, herbs, vegetables, dairy and so forth.

"Be increasingly wary of the quality of food you eat. Acquire food from sources that you know to be true to na-

ture. *Buy locally-grown and organic foods, and avoid ge-
netically-engineered foods. As often as possible, grow your
own food.*

"*Do not eat or prepare food while you are upset in any
way or while watching television. This consciousness pene-
trates the food, and you may not be able to assimilate it in a
healthy manner. Be aware of others preparing food. Food
has consciousness and picks up the vibrational energy of
those who prepare it. If you are not aware of who prepared
the food, such as when you eat out or when you buy processed food at the grocery store, bless the food with prayer
and give it healing energy to make it whole.*"

"I like to tell people that I grocery shop the periphery.
The periphery is around the inside walls of the grocery
store. That is where the dairy, fruits and vegetables are.
These are the healthier things to buy. Most processed foods
are on the innermost shelves and are not as healthy for
you."

"*Good idea! Why didn't I think of that?*"

"Pretty funny! 1 Corinthians, 3:16 reads, 'Do you not
know that you are God's temple and that God's Spirit
dwells in you?' Does this mean my physical body?"

"*Mankind often interprets this as meaning that the body
itself is the temple. It is a fanciful thought that the temple
God dwells in is your disposable physical body, as if it
were a structure. You are so much more than your body.
The temple God lives in is YOU, as a whole being, of body
and mind and soul. So, therefore, you must not only care*

for your body but also for your mind and soul. When you die, your physical body deteriorates. After death, the Spirit of God continues to live on in you as mind and soul."

"Several years ago, I took a class on how to heal with love by working through the heart chakra. It is amazing how love can really change things. We took two decanters of water. Doing nothing to one decanter, we held our hands over the other decanter. Prayerfully, we sent the water love by breathing in, holding the breath in the heart and filling it with love, then sending the breath down our arms and out our hands, directing the love into the water. We did this for about five minutes. Loving energy entered the water, and love changed the taste! The taste difference was remarkable. The energized water was sweeter! It reminded me of when you changed the water into wine."

"Precisely! In ancient times, hands were placed over the food and a prayerful intention was said. Loving, healing energy was purposely invoked into the food, while becoming one with it, making it healthier and holier for consumption. This custom has lost its meaning. Now most people say a short mealtime prayer without seriously thinking about consciously sending healing, loving energy into the food to make it healthy and whole. They don't realize the power of loving, healing energy. You must become the prayer. Invoke purifying, loving energy into all food you partake of or prepare. Practice so that it becomes habit. It does not take fanfare and noisy show, just pure simplicity of the intention to purify, and knowing it is so."

"I always tell people that the power of prayer for purifying food or in healing is enhanced by the use of hands held over the food or directed at someone in healing. Energy flows naturally through the hands and through the palm chakra. That is the reasoning behind the ancient custom of holding your hands over food while blessing it or 'laying on of hands.' I like to teach others how to feel this energy between their own hands. So I ask you, the reader, to dry your hands thoroughly, then rub them together for half a minute. Hold your hands about six inches apart, palm facing palm. Pretend you have a small ball between your hands and feel the energy of the ball, while moving your hands away from the ball and then into it, again and again. You may be able to feel energy between your palms or even your fingertips. This is the energy of the aura that is within you and around you. Eventually, with practice, without rubbing your hands together, you will be able to feel this energy surrounding every area of your body or another's, around plants, animals and even minerals.

"Someone once said that, if you had the foulest food, you could make it safe to eat by sending loving energy into it."

Laughing, Jesus said, *"Only try that if you are starving. For it is only if you can consciously focus on your oneness with the food, that change and miracles happen."*

"Some time ago, I invited a daughter, her boy friend, his mother and my granddaughter over for dinner. We sat down to eat and I asked who would like to say grace. Jokingly one said, 'Grace.' My granddaughter, who was seven years old at that time, was sitting very contemplatively

through the giggling and said softly, 'I think I can do this.'
In her own words, she proceeded to say a beautiful prayer
of thanksgiving. We were humbled and touched by her
sweetness. It reminded me of the Bible passage that says,
'And a little child shall lead them.'"

*"Ah . . . the children. . . . Follow her example. This child
is blessed. Energize your food with loving, healing energy
and always say a prayer of thanksgiving. Your foods are
being drained of minerals and vitamins and contain many
contaminants. Prayer energizes the food and makes it
whole. While in this physical consciousness, do not put one
morsel of food into your body without first loving it, and
then give it as an offering to your temple."*

"What of fasting?"

*"Sweet fasting. . . . Within the meditative mind lies the
health of your body. Refreshment lies in the heart and soul.
The reason for fasting must come from the heart. Fasting
for physical health should be limited to no more than three
days. Fasting for cleansing of mind and spirit can be of
longer duration."*

"I once set my mind to fast for ten days. During this
time, I drank water, with lemon juice, a little cayenne pep-
per and maple syrup in it. The first three days were difficult, but I stuck with it. After that I had no difficulty at all.
On my ninth day, I was invited to a birthday party in a restaurant. I ordered herb tea and, when it came, I could not
taste it, so I just set it aside. Then I thought I would order a
different flavor of tea. Still I could not taste it. The birthday

person, sitting alongside of me, told me to order a cup of hot water and he would fix me a tea I could surely taste. So the waitress brought me a cup of steaming water. Into the water my friend put a teaspoon of perfumed vibhuti (sacred ash). Initially, I could not get it up to my mouth. I was overcome by a fragrance so powerful that it nearly knocked me over. I inhaled it over and over. I could taste the vibhuti before I even put the tea to my lips. Then slowly I drank it. My taste buds were working overtime, trying to keep up with the taste of the fragrance. I wanted everyone to try it, but no one seemed as enthusiastic as I. I was filled with indescribable bliss.

"I broke my fast on the eleventh day, and I was ready and hungry. I really think, now, that if I had set my mind to fast for forty days and nights, I could have done it. But I had set in my mind that I would fast for ten days, and that is how long my hunger abated!"

"The power of the mind is strong. Mind over matter is exactly that. Use your mind to control your body. Food is secondary in caring for your body. Give it only what it needs, not always what it wants."

"Thank you, Sweet Jesus. I am honored by your presence in my life."

Chapter Five

War

What causes wars, and what causes fightings among you?
Is it not your passions that are at war in your members?
You desire and do not have; so you kill.
And you covet and cannot obtain; so you fight and wage war.
You do not have, because you do not ask.
You ask and do not receive, because you ask wrongly,
to spend it on your passions.

—James (4: 01-03)

"Sweet Jesus, is it a sin to kill in war?"

"Thou shalt not kill. War, among other things, is cause and effect, resulting from and in karmic debt. Karmic experiences are destined to happen over and over, unless the chains of karma are broken and love reigns. The commandment 'Thou shalt not kill,' along with love, non-violence and forgiveness, would rid the earth of this karma, and world-wide peace would be maintained for generations to come.

"In the meantime, war continues to exist because of mankind's misuse of free will. If a country or individual feels they must go to war, it has to be done only for the sake of a higher cause such as preserving true freedom and true equality of mankind, and even then, done without malice or seeking vengeance.

"Remember the heroes of nine-eleven. In one of many heroic acts, your countrymen, women and children unhesitatingly diverted a plane and died to save the life of your president and many others. That was unconditional love, in that immediate, present moment, pure and simple."

My husband, George, and I were overwhelmed with this reminder of that historic day. I am amazed that Jesus would even talk of war and killing the enemy. I always thought He advocated total non-violence. No killing for any reason. George felt that what Jesus said did not alter His opposition to violence.

"Vengeful acts result in like karma. As I said, only through love, non-violence and forgiveness can these sins be karmically eliminated.

"To start with, all weapons of mass destruction in all countries must be contained and destroyed: biological, nuclear, genetic. I'm not talking only about countries that are deemed dangerous. I am talking about all countries. You must stem the tide that could wipe out humanity. There is too much at stake."

"Do you mean to render a country defenseless!?"

"If all were to live in love, there would be no need to de-

fend. There is presently a momentum of war and terrorism that has to be stopped. Eradicating the means to defend, within all countries and especially those that are threatening the world with terrorism, is the most humane way to end war. If mankind, working together as one under a whole-world order, cannot eliminate war and terrorism, the world as you know it will remain in this cycle forever.

"Work for peace and non-violence with all mankind. Pray for world peace in all of your prayers. Human life is precious. True power lies in the power of love, not in weapons.

"Does it make sense that whole nations are killing each other over religion, greed and power? Listen carefully to what I say . . . all religions must be based on love toward all mankind, or they simply are not a religion. Religions that support vengeance, malice, or prejudice are not godly. Countries that give rise to war have war within their boundaries. Countries and religions that break with terror grow in peace. True freedom and true equality are determined according to God's law, not the law of fanatic religious leaders or the greedy."

"Sweet Jesus, why would anyone want to become a terrorist? I cannot even imagine doing such a thing."

"Terrorists are desperate men, women and children from off the street. They are grateful for the companionship and the sustenance, and through conditioning, they readily do and believe what they are told. Some have seen so many acts of violence that they feel they need to fight back, and terrorism, they think, is the only way they can make a dif-

ference. Some are simply forced into combat and cannot find the means to escape.

"Terrorism is being fueled by some religious and secular groups still living in the lower dimensions, who believe in a vengeful God. They teach vengeance to the hopeless and lead them to believe that this kind of martyrdom will take them direct to God. This is untruth!

"In the Old Testament, in Leviticus, God said, 'You shall not take vengeance or bear a grudge, but you shall love your neighbor as yourself.' I tell you, you must learn to retaliate with love, not malice, even in war. Strive to love unconditionally, in all situations. Fill every present moment with love."

"Killing is bad enough, but to kill because you think it is the way to God is . . . well, I can't even think of a word here. It's beyond my ability to contemplate that possibility."

"Saint Ta, in your occupational therapy career, you studied and worked with developmental progressions, and you have since studied physical, chakra and auric energy. Since you understand developmental progressions, I would like to use those concepts to make some things easier for you to understand.

"Mankind has countless developmental progressions: progressions in the womb, childhood developmental progressions, progressions in body chemistry, progressions for learning, for aging, for emotional and spiritual growth, chakra progressions and many more.

"So too, does this concept apply to group consciousness.

Through religious and personal beliefs, terrorists, as a group, are still seeing a God of vengeance, as was often portrayed in the Old Testament by man. Many are still in the lower chakratic—vengeful, survivalistic—dimensions in their spiritual developmental progression.

"There are those born into these lower dimensions who do not learn of a loving God. They may be thirsty, hungry and poor. They may be uneducated. They may see and envy all that you have. They may feel cornered and come out fighting, and have no care for their own lives because they do not have any hope left. They are the ones that are promised salvation through their religions, not God's, if they sacrifice their lives as martyrs. They are a threat to the rest of mankind and the environment.

"I was born to give light unto the world and bring mankind out of the lower dimensions toward a loving God. Progress for most has since been easier."

There were many more questions unasked that this conversation raised. Every time I tried to put the questions into words, none came. Only thoughts scattered into nothingness. It was as if Jesus was scrambling my mind, only allowing questions He was willing to answer. Yet I realized what He shared with me was profound.

After a time, I went on, "What can we do?"

"Terrorism is the result of inequalities and hopelessness, which need to be addressed so that our free will will lead to love and peace. Provide empowerment to all people through education and jobs with living wages. Pray unceasingly for peace and the good of all mankind. Turn it

over to God. Meditate daily. Go inward. Love all actions. Thank God, praise God and, above all, TRUST in God and know God is a loving God."

"Are you saying we should love all actions, even violence?"

"Yes. Love is the only chance for peace and is the best of all weapons. Love your enemies and pray for those who persecute you, so that you may be sons of your Father who is in heaven, for He makes the sun rise on the evil and on the good, and sends rain on the just and on the unjust. If you love those who love you, what reward have you? Love your enemy, and change will happen."

"How can we love them?"

"Center yourself in the present moment as you pray. Listen when I say . . . that many disasters have been diverted by sending love and prayer to perceived enemies. Remember, the energy of loving thoughts counteracts evil.

"Countries that are dedicated to the preservation of the right of physical, mental and spiritual growth of all of their citizens radiate love, and good follows. These countries, as group consciousness, have the responsibility of generating this love to others on earth.

"Countries that condone inequality within their borders will continue to have karmic disharmony until change occurs. Pray daily for all leaders, so they keep love and balance uppermost in their minds when considering the difficult responsibilities that they have to deal with.

"Imagine if you will, if whole nations could learn to live

in each present moment with love, with all the past for-
given, there would be no war and no terrorism. Ego's
greed for power must be reversed, and world leadership
must be given to those who truly want peace and equality.
All countries should be separate, and yet part of a whole-
world order."

"One world under God, with liberty and justice for all."

"Sounds really good, doesn't it."

"Sounds so American—one world under God, with liberty and justice for all—but this is the hope of the world.
There is so much anti-Americanism in many parts of the
world. What can we do about that?"

"It is easy to have a loving God when things are going
well for you. It is much harder to find a loving God when
you are hungry and starving and watching your children
die, while hearing about the wealth of others.

"It is only through the continued love and generosity of
America and her citizens that you will win back good will.
You must all, individually and as a nation, set a loving ex-
ample for the rest of the world. Many of you are so over-
whelmed by the needs of others that you do nothing. You
are wanna-be saviors of the whole world, but your world
revolves around you. Remember, I said, 'Pick a charity,
need, or project.' Start there. It is everyone working to-
gether that makes a whole. Put yourself into it, send money,
give of your time. Prayer makes a difference, too. If every-
one, no matter how young or old, did something, the world
would be a better place.

"As more and more of mankind becomes able to live in love, forgiveness and equality with their fellow man, group consciousness will change, and love and peace will endure, and heaven on earth will be evident. No bad karma for man or group consciousness can exist where love, forgiveness and equalities dwell."

"Is it too late to start over to help educate these people, or feed their hungry, or find jobs for them to earn money? There is so much inequality."

"It is never too late to start over. Sound education, from early childhood to the elderly, is always good and empowers people to help themselves. Educators will be needed.

"There are some people who do not have any access to food in their vicinity. There are whole areas of starvation and no sanitation or water. Yet, even in these areas, people share what little they have. Often it is the poor who help the poor. The poor are more open to giving and sharing than those who have wealth. Their gifts of sharing with each other are greater because that is all they have. Some poor people give all they have every day of their lives.

"Those that hoard money for selfish purposes and do not share it with the less fortunate are not storing up treasures for heaven, for it is the love of money that is evil. Blessed are those who give to the poor and needy, for they shall not know hunger. You have wanted to give to a charity for children. Do it; share your blessings."

"Some people don't believe in giving to charity, thinking their money will not go to the people who need it."

"There are many charities that are legitimate. One just needs to do a little research and then unconditionally do it. Surrender the money to God. Put it in His hands.

"Many are the miracles that happen in everyday life while humanity administers to the poor and hungry, sick and needy. It is never too late. Life is precious, right down to the last physical breath. When love is given through aid, good comes of it. If you are unable to give money, give of your time to raise money or to work with the needy. If you are unable to give money and are unable to physically help, pray, and send love and light to where it is needed. Intuitively, you know where you are needed and what you can do. Do not be disillusioned by lack of stability, much time will be invested by all to regain stability. I say, do not give up on humanity. Life is precious. It is never too late."

"Can the war on violence be won?"

"All things are possible, but first, the basic needs of all people have to be addressed, as these inequalities only breed jealousy, anger, and dissatisfaction towards those who have more, and sometimes this leads to terrorism.

"It is most important to get at the core of all issues. Your world is getting smaller and smaller from the fast pace you live. You can jet to the other side of your earth in the same day. Your television gives you immediate international news you would not be aware of without this access. Sometimes distorted—still, this news brings all nations closer and closer to each other.

"Love thy neighbor. Ask what you can do for your neighbor. Learn to live in the present moment at your heart

level, and then you can settle problems before they get to be at the mind level. If everyone could practice and learn to do this, soon whole countries could do this."

"With all of these prayers, love and light, why aren't terrorists at bay?"

"You must realize things would be much worse without all the prayers and healing."

"Sweet Jesus, is there hope? What about our future?"

"I cannot predict the future; no one can. Predictions constantly change with prayer and love. Do not believe all the predictions that you hear. Only guesses and generalities can be made. Pray for peace. There is always hope. Help comes in many ways. Great assistance is pouring into all the earth. Terror will diminish and wars will end.

"I tell you, do not give up on humanity or yourself. Be willing to aid those less fortunate, in any way you can. Display tenderness toward all who suffer. Develop gentleness and soft answers. Have patience, and above all, an abiding love for those who cross your path."

"Our nations seem to be existing on a fine line. Our monetary systems are unstable, viruses are unpredictable, and violence still exists. Shouldn't we, as individuals, start to prepare for survival, in our own homes and communities? We could freeze, can, and store up food. . . ."

Jesus didn't give me time to finish. Interrupting me, He emphatically said, *"It is crucial, at this time, for all people to be strong and positive in their love for their country and to not lose faith. Negativity can only sprout more negativ-*

ity. Your country is so materialistic that you count on many things, based on your monetary system. That is not the only way. Bartering and co-ops are going to be available for just about anything you might need. Just know that God will provide. I don't mean you should lie around and expect God to show up and care for you. God will provide you with the means to survive. It might mean a job, or aid, or the ability to be self-sustaining. Do not give up on your country; it has a strong foundation.

"You do not need everything that you think you do. And many of you worry for no reason at all. There are many, many more people living in poor conditions than people who are able to buy food at a store. Many are not so confident that food will show up.

"Prepare as you see fit. When I say this, I don't say it lightly. And remember, it is also good to store up treasures for heaven by doing good acts and loving everyone."

"Jesus, speaking of worry, you said, in the beginning of these writings, that people are afraid and times are rough. Can you tell us more about the future? There is so much fear and violence and terrorism. What are we to expect? How can we cope?"

"Like-energy magnetically attracts like-energy. Fear attracts that which you fear most. When personal, group, or national fears build, it creates even further fearful thoughts and actions. Fear stifles the imagination and suppresses ambition. It is only through love, prayer and positive thinking and actions, that many disasters have been diverted, and change occurred for the better.

"It is easy for me to ask of you to have faith in God and expect miracles, to go within and meditate on the wonders of God, and to praise and thank God for all your many blessings. But it is your initiative as individuals—alone or gathered together, living in love—that will make change happen to bring about world peace and heaven on earth.

"Tell me, Sweet Jesus, where did all of this evil come from in the first place? Some say God created evil."

"Out of ignorance, mankind uses free will to gain power over each other in corrupt ways, creating evil. In order for humanity to fulfill the universal law of oneness and to transform this precious planet into Heaven on Earth, you must own the fact that it is mankind's free will that causes evil. Eliminate the inconceivable belief that God created evil."

"You mean humans are the cause of evil on earth?"

"Evil, as you understand it, is a term for mankind's desecration of free will in your physical and creative faculties of thought, feeling and action."

"What about earth changes—earthquakes and so forth?"

"What about them?"

"Well . . . they cause hardship for so many people and so many lives are lost. Is Mother Earth cleansing herself? Is man causing it through evil?"

"As I said before, there are cycles in creation that give strength when what you perceive is doom or evil. All of creation is in cycles, including mankind and Mother Earth.

The cycles are constantly cleansing and rebuilding, just like breathing out and breathing in is cleansing for your physical body. It is not evil. It is natural and full of God's love. Do you remember, I told you what you perceive as evil is often not what you perceive it to be? If you could remember your divinity, you would see all things with love."

"How can we remember our divinity?

"Living in non-judgmental oneness is the beginning of remembering your divinity. There are no distinctions in oneness—only perfection—as all is one. Oppositions and evil vanish. Yogananda will speak to you at length about becoming consciously aware of changeless consciousness (oneness), in your next book."

"I can't help but think about the quantum leap from this earth plane consciousness to always living in the oneness of God. Wouldn't it be wonderful if we could realize, all the time, that we are one."

"Saint Ta . . . the majority of mankind defines their selves as separate, instead of unified in reality in the eternal now. As individuals become more attuned to all as one, they will attract more and more individuals to this realization. Remember, like-energy magnetically attracts like-energy."

"The sun and moon, and good and evil—opposites. . . . Everything seems to have an opposite—a duality, a negative. How can they be one?"

"Ah, Saint Ta . . . there is nothing negative or evil about

the moon. Opposites do not indicate negativity. Opposites were created for harmonious balance in your perceived world and so that you might experience the sun and the moon, and the good and the evil, and all other dualities until you come to realize that all is one and there is nothing to compare. The lesson is in that realization. On earth there will always be the illusion of opposites by those who are unable to embrace the realization that all things are unified as one."

"We are taught the energy in the universe is finite—redistribution occurs, but none is made or destroyed. So . . . is this true with good and evil? Light and dark? Love and hate? Is there a finite and unchangeable amount of either? Or, for instance, can more love be created and an equal amount less of hate? Or can either be added or deleted independent of the other? Are we to always count on having love and hate, and the balance will always be love in some areas and hate in other areas of our world, constantly changing back and forth between the two, but the united total never increasing or decreasing?"

"Within the vastness of God there are universes of universes. Do not put limits on God. God is love and is infinite and omnipresent, even unto the ends of the worlds, and love has no opposites nor comparisons."

"So the possibility of a world filled with love absent of evil exists?"

"Definitely. The world is already filled with love.

"It is only in your own perceived containment, that you

have created and become caught up in what you understand to be good and evil by your comparisons and judgments. Mankind judges one as being better than the other when, in reality, you created the experience of both, making each only possible in the presence of the other.

"New energies are created daily, ever-changing, uncontained, into the infinite. God is limitless. Creation is not in the past. Creation is as in the present as you are, and more limitless than you can even imagine.

"To find the divinity in all things as one, you must go beyond judgment and comparisons, and acknowledge the possibility that all is unified in love as one, even the perceived evil. And, in this spiritual growth, you will catch glimpses into the real world, where only ever-expanding love prevails.

"If you light a candle in the darkness, radiant light shines forth. The darkness becomes one with the light. And when the light goes out, the light becomes one with the darkness. When all of humanity learns to realize and experience all situations in God-consciousness as one, wars will cease and the new Heaven on Earth will be born."

"Some say evil opposes love . . ."

I couldn't even get the sentence finished when Jesus emphatically said, *"Love has no opposites and no opponents! God is love! Love embraces all, including evil. As I said before, through the desecration of free will in your physical and creative faculties of thought, feeling and action, mankind created perceived evil. God, as love, is ever-present, embracing all as one.*

"All realms, heavens and creation abide in oneness with God—of pure love, absent of vengeance. Through your prayers and goodness, this omniscient, omnipotent, omnipresent God of love may intervene in all matters of unlimited, universal creation.

"Think of it as one world—in which you, God, and all creation exist as one—embracing all of humankind's misconceptions, delusions, evil tendencies, love and terrorism. When you can see the One, you will experience all as divine love."

"There is so much mystery . . . dichotomies, dualism, oneness . . . confusing."

"If the mysteries of God were explained to all of humanity, they would still want to know 'WHY?' Many times answers are given, and still the question 'WHY?' is unendingly asked, over and over. One answer is not the right answer for all of humanity, nor for all time. God is limitless and ever-creating. Many things must be left to mystery."

I bowed my head for a moment, relaxed my whole body, took a deep breath and sighed. I could hear a deep resonance, like the sound of the deep, sustained Om. . . .

Continuing on, I asked, "How can we help children cope?"

"It is important to teach all the children that God, or that I, Jesus, or another master is their friend. Tell them . . . 'No one can take God away. Not war. Not terrorism. Not death. God lives everywhere and is with you always.'

"And tell them for me . . . 'When you are afraid, cross

*your heart with your hands and hold yourself in a big hug,
and imagine that God or I or another master is holding
you, because we are. And fear not. Crossing your heart into
a hug is something you always have with you. If your hands
are not free, imagine, with your creative mind, that I am
holding you, because I am. If you are weak and sick, imagine with your creative mind that I am holding you, because
I am. I am wrapping you in my robe with my arms and
holding you close to my heart. Lay your head gently upon
my bosom and I shall give you rest.'"*

"That is so beautiful. . . ."

I rested in those thoughts for a while. It brought back
memories of our friend, Victor, who died of cancer. In the
end stages, he would hold his hands tightly across his heart
in an embrace. He said it was the one comfort that he had,
and he was sure God was holding him. He knew.

"It reminds me, too, of a song I used to sing as a small
child. I always felt comforted when I sang it."

> Come into my heart.
> Come into my heart.
> Come into my heart, Lord Jesus.
> Come in today.
> Come in to stay.
> Come into my heart, Lord Jesus.

*"Children are especially vulnerable to neglect, abuse
and terrorism because they are often unable to control
their situation, as are many adults. Children have fears that
you don't understand and they don't know how to express.
They cry aloud into their early years. Being born into the*

earth plane and, seemingly, separate from God, children often long for God in their crying. They may not recognize what it is they long for. Even adults have longings they can't quite understand.

"Children are also more open to laughter, because they are so newly-released from God and they have memory of the bliss. Children and adults should not be stifled in their crying or laughter.

"Parents should be selective in what they expose their children to. Limit television use. It is never good to keep things from a child totally. They need to be able to ask questions and get honest answers. Do not lie to them. Explain to them simply and with few words, in their language, what is going on in the world, when they ask. If they appear to be avoiding the situations completely, then question them to get them talking. It is important to be able to communicate feelings. Children are beautiful. Listen to them; take time for them."

"Ah, Sweet Jesus, that reminds me of some children in my life right now who are extraordinary. One visits the retreat every Sunday with his grandmother. He has an attention-deficit disorder and is very active, and yet, has brought joy to our lives. He likes to put both of his hands on each side of my face, then he carefully puts his forehead upon my forehead, and we exchange a very beautiful energy. Then he thanks me and I thank him. He does this with others, too.

"Recently, my whole family was together at a restaurant to celebrate the birthday of my mother. A granddaughter got up from where she was eating, at another table, and came to where I was sitting, and did the same thing to me.

Placed her hands on both sides of my face and brought her forehead to meet mine. Then she backed off, her eyes wide open with surprise, only to come back for more. In that moment, there was profound energy. And then, satisfied, she returned to her place at the table."

"These children are a light unto the world. They are seeking energy. They will know, by this act, who they can receive energy from and will be drawn to these persons to do this act over and over. They may test others who will not give them what they need, and they will move on, constantly searching. Be ever ready and watchful."

"Recently, this same granddaughter was sitting at the dinner table, and her mother suddenly said to her, 'What is wrong with you?' And she said, 'I don't know. I get these shivers going up and down my spine!' I immediately sensed its importance. I asked her, 'How long has this been going on?' She answered, 'Oh, for a couple of years now.' I asked, 'How does it feel?' With a smile, she answered, 'Real good.' I asked, 'Where does it start from?' 'From the bottom of my spine to the top of my head.' 'What causes it?' 'I don't know, it just happens.'"

"This is Spirit, beginning to awaken her energy centers. It is happening to many children everywhere. Once they set aside their childish ways, they may show the potential to be spiritual leaders of this age.

"In the meantime, the children must be allowed to be children. You can teach and steer them and be their beacon of light, but you must let them be their selves. They will find their way."

We paused here. . . . Then time simply faded. It was as if there was nothing . . . no thoughts, no sound, no body movement. I suddenly realized I was out of my body and suspended above our large globe, close enough to distinguish land masses. I was sending peace and love through light to terrorists, refugees, victims, new leaders around the world, and all those caught up in war. I could not differentiate between enemy and ally; they were all one. I could sense many other light workers. I could not see them; I just knew they were there. After a time, there was nothingness once again, and then I was back in ordinary consciousness.

Oh . . . that we could save this world for all the beautiful children. . . .

Chapter Six

Healing

Now there are varieties of gifts, but the same Spirit;
and there are varieties of service, but the same Lord;
and there are varieties of working,
but it is the same God who inspires them all in every one.

To each is given the manifestation of the Spirit
for the common good.

To one is given through the Spirit the utterance of wisdom,
and to another the utterance of knowledge
according to the same Spirit,
to another faith by the same Spirit,
to another gifts of healing by the one Spirit,
to another the working of miracles, to another prophecy,
to another the ability to distinguish between spirits,
to another various kinds of tongues,
to another the interpretation of tongues.

All these are inspired by one and the same Spirit,
who apportions to each one individually as he wills.

—1 Corinthians 12: 4 -11

My conversations with Jesus are mostly in the very early hours of the morning. I never know where they are going to lead, but I eagerly look forward to them, because they always bring new discoveries and joys. Maybe that is why, when I go to bed at night, I can hardly wait for morning to arrive.

Seven years ago, I had thoroughly cleaned and put my house in order before leaving for my first assignment as a traveling occupational therapist. As I entered my car to leave, I was suddenly compelled to go back into the house. It was a beautiful home, situated on the Manistee river, within view of Lake Michigan. I walked back in, looked into every room, looked out the windows upon my beloved river, said my good-byes, then satisfied, I started to leave. Turning around at the door for one last look, I said to myself, "I can die now." I didn't know then, but now it is clear to me that my old way of living and thinking died, for it was on that first assignment that I was made aware of my healing gift.

Talking to the ever-present Jesus, I said, "People often ask me how I became a healer and how it all started."

"It began many lifetimes ago."

"But it took me a while to recognize my healing gift in this lifetime. It was a physical therapist who made me aware of my healing abilities. Through his direction I was able to feel my aura. I had never heard about auras! I didn't even know what they were. He told me that, when I was at home and relaxed in bed, I should reach out and gently bring my hands in toward my body and try to feel differences in the air. 'That,' he said, 'is the aura.' Surprisingly, I did find differences in the air.

"I had a backache at the time. The physical therapist did not tell me to feel the aura and heal myself; however, something told me to smooth out the aura in the area of my back. I did and the backache left. When I went to work the next morning, I didn't even bring the subject up. I guess I needed another lesson. It came quickly enough.

"Within a few days, I had an earache that did not let up. I knew I needed to go to a doctor to get antibiotics for it. In the meantime, the backache showed up again. I lay down on the floor to alleviate the pain. While there, I remembered what had happened a few nights prior. So I reached out, felt the aura, and smoothed it out. Once again, the backache was gone. Then, I thought to myself, 'Well, I might as well fix my ears while I'm down here!' So I made a few swipes to clear the air around my ears and the earache was instantly gone! I couldn't believe it. I lay there, thinking that, if I moved, it would come back. Soon the phone rang. I don't remember who called, but I do remember that the pain was gone even after jumping up to get the phone. Really gone. After talking to whomever it was on the phone, I phoned my pastor back home and asked him if he was sitting down. Then I told him what had happened. He hesitantly and carefully said to me, 'It is a gift. However, be careful how you use it or they will burn you at the stake!' I immediately realized the implications of what had happened.

"That evening in my prayers, and many times after that, I asked the question: 'What do you want me to do now,

Lord?' I was a conservative Lutheran and I was having a hard time dealing with the concept of being a healer. I was not questioning its validity. I just wanted to know what was expected of me, and if I would be able to follow through with whatever God wanted me to do.

"During this time, while I was working as a hand therapist in a rehabilitation clinic, a young man came in for therapy. He had had brain stem surgery and was unable to lie down or even lean his head forward, sideways, or backward without feeling dizzy or nauseated. He was rigid, unshaven, unkempt, walked with a cane, and he had his father with him. Since the hand clinic did not have a set-up for the kind of gross motor therapy he would require, I wondered why the doctor would send him to me. With this wondering came the feeling that I was supposed to heal him. In my innocence, I proceeded, totally led by intuition and God. I didn't say anything to him or his father about what my thoughts were. I simply asked him to sit still while I first massaged his neck. I then told him I would be continuing, but he wouldn't feel anything. While his father sat motionless on a chair at our side, I allowed Spirit to guide me. I held my hands off his head at the crown. I felt his aura and immediately experienced a beautiful connectedness with this young man. I had never felt an aura on anyone else before. A prayer came to me, as if out of nowhere, first praising and then asking for guidance, protection for both myself and for the young man, and healing for his highest good.

"In the silent, loving joy that I felt, paying no attention to his father sitting at our side, I smoothed out the heaviness in his aura. I grabbed and tossed, and erased what needed to be removed from his energy field. Then, suddenly, I felt done with it.

"I told him to lay his head down on my desk. I asked him if he was dizzy or nauseated. 'No,' he said. I told him to lie down on a bench. I asked him if he was dizzy or nauseated. 'No.' I told him to get down on his hands and knees and rock back and forth as fast as he could. I asked him if he was dizzy or nauseated. 'No.' I sent him home.

"When he came in for his next appointment, he was clean-shaven, dressed impeccably, no cane and shining. With his father behind him, he walked up to me and said, 'I don't know what you did to me the other day, but there is nothing wrong with me now.' I literally stopped in my tracks. So many things went through my mind as I discharged him from therapy. Again, I couldn't help but wonder what God had in store for me. That was the first healing I was involved in of someone other than myself, and just the beginning."

"While in the embrace of The Divine, many blessings are given to newly-realized healers. Just as a newborn baby has a special immunity to viruses, in the beginning, to give her or him a good start in life, so does a newly-realized healer have a built-in immunity to outside influences. In their innocence they do not concentrate long on the what and why of it all. They do not attract what they do not know. If healers could only maintain that mentality instead of getting so analytical and boastful of their gift, even more profound healings would take place."

From there I went to St. Louis. I had little to do with the decision. St. Louis is a very large city and I don't like large cities.

My three-month assignment was in a skilled nursing home. I was not allowed to use my new healing gift in this setting. However, some patients were suddenly sleeping better or had less pain, and they seemed to sense why and sought me out. They would wheel their wheelchairs into where I was doing therapy and ask for hands on. They passed the word around.

I attended a small Lutheran church outside of St. Louis for the duration of my assignment. One evening, they were having a pancake supper, and I was eager for some socialization apart from working in my new setting. When I entered the church vestibule, I saw there were many posters with pictures of a baby on them. This was a fund-raiser for a family burdened by major medical bills because their baby had serious physical problems. He had had a high fever that resulted in loss of ability to digest and propel food and eliminate waste from his body. I was mesmerized by the pictures and felt moved to go see this baby.

A few days later, I called and went in to see the pastor. I told him of my new-found gift for healing and that I would like to go see this baby. He thought that would be fine. However, the baby was the center of some media attention. Doctors from across the country were trying to solve his problems. I did not want any part of the media, so I chose to try long-distance healing with visualization and healing prayer, imagining the baby on my lap. At the time, I had not been taught such a procedure. All instruction came from intuition and God.

In the evening, I would imagine this small baby on my lap, and I would scan his body. I found discrepancies in his aura in the stomach area and smoothed them out, not really considering if it was doing any good. It just seemed as if I knew everything was going to be all right.

At the end of my three-month assignment, when I had three weeks left, I suddenly felt it all-important to go see the little one, an urgency I could not ignore. So I called the pastor again, and he made arrangements to swear the family to secrecy, no media, and to go with me.

It was the way I had imagined it. The baby was hooked up to many devices. He was being fed through the heart and, having been on steroids, was huge and hairy. I held him on my lap, tubes and all, and scanned his body, and found heaviness in exactly the same area as in my visualized treatments.

I worked with him every day for one week, and by the end of the week, I knew he was healed. His mother and sister received treatments also. She told me that from day one, when I arrived at their home, they all started sleeping the whole night through. Prior to that, none of them could sleep through the night.

The second week, I went three times, basically for the mother. My feeling was that the baby did not need me any more. I couldn't say this to the mother, as his problem was all internal and couldn't be visually verified.

The third week, I only went twice. The mother said she would be taking the baby in for tests after Mother's Day and that I could call her then to find out what the results were.

When I left St. Louis, the church presented me with a beautiful cross, which was the first thing I unpacked and put up when I arrived in New Mexico on my next assignment. It went with me for the three years I worked at assignments across the country. Now it is on a wall between the sliding doors in our living room.

Just before Mother's Day, I called the mother to wish her a happy Mother's Day. I wasn't calling to find out about the test results, since I knew she wasn't supposed to have them yet. She shouted excitedly in my ear, "I have been trying to find you. We took the baby in early for tests, and they are now starting to wean him off steroids and are starting to give him some foods by mouth!"

The last time I went through St. Louis, I couldn't see the baby. He was out watching a parade!

"Sweet Jesus, God and You were with me through all of my traveling assignments across the country. With You, I was able to come to terms with the gift, and healing became my way of life. I doubt I could have done it alone."

"Saint Ta, God and I are always within you. . . ."

"God told me not to study or read about healing and, for two years, I didn't. Everyone wanted me to read this book or that book and to study different techniques. Yet, everything came from God as I needed it. Why would I have wanted someone else to give me advice? There were lessons everywhere . . ."

". . . and from within yourself. And you accepted it with love, Saint Ta. The love you have in your heart for this

work has been unconditional and beautiful. If you had started out studying, you would have been floundering out there, grasping for straws, wondering, 'What do I do next?' But you simply listened intuitively, and you let God lead you."

"While on assignment in New Mexico, I was working with a woman who had cancer. I wanted her healed so badly. She was young, had a loving family, and I wanted her well. I realized, in the healing process, the point at which her breast cancer left, but I could not shake her of the lymphatic cancer throughout her body. I would get physically sick when I worked with her. At that time I was not studying anything and couldn't figure out why this would happen to me. The pastor in the church I attended recommended I go see a healer in Ruidoso, who also teaches 'Healing Touch.' So I finally made the appointment and went to see her. I arrived and knocked on the door. She opened it and exclaimed, 'I can't see you right now; I am feeding my husband.' As she pointed out of the door, she continued, 'Take a walk down that path and come back in a little while.' Slam went the door.

"Feeling like I really wanted to leave, I nevertheless was moved to do as she said. I looked around for the path and found that it followed a ridge of the mountain. I walked for a while and discovered a fire site with seats all around. I wasn't interested in staying there, but I was moved to walk off the path and go a short way down the mountainside. I soon came upon an enormous amount of stirring energy in the air surrounding me. I stopped and sat down, and began to 'dance with the spirits.' As I swayed, merged and played with the spirits in the air, I could hear music with drumming and felt a wonderful sense of joy as the spirits danced on and on with me. When I opened my eyes, I realized that I was sitting in the midst of, and facing, a semi-circle of many mounds! Old, decayed tree trunks lined the front and back of each mound.

"I continued my joyful dance for a while and then, suddenly, I realized the healer was behind me, watching. I stood up and she reverently said, 'You do me and our mountain honor by being here.' With no hesitation, I said, 'I didn't know that anyone could own an Indian burial ground.' She said, 'We don't; we are just caretakers.' As we started back on the path, I remember feeling as if I were walking on sacred ground. It was almost as if I were stepping on the past. I was totally at one with the earth, and I carefully picked where I would place my feet as I walked. As we walked, words tumbled out of my mouth, seemingly coming from nowhere. I asked, 'What is the difference between Indian spiritualism and Christianity?' She answered, 'They are one and the same.' I asked her to understand that I was not studying anything at this time, but I had a specific problem I needed an answer to. I then proceeded to tell her why I came, asking her why I get sick when I work with my client. She answered, 'That is simple. You are not letting go and letting God. You want her healed so badly that you are desperate to do the healing. It is making you sick. Just let go and let God.' I visited with her for a short time, thanked her, and left.

"Over time, we became friends. God provided me with a beautiful lesson and a beautiful friend. Since then I have been able to let go and let God do the work, and I don't get sick.

"Being a healer has often been challenging, especially since I started out as a conservative Christian. It amazes me, now, that the Christian community does not always accept healers. Some of them shun healers and have little faith in the healing arts."

"Skepticism is not limited to Christians. Those who are skeptical have not realized God gave gifts of healing, working of miracles, words of wisdom, knowledge, faith, prophecy, distinguishing between spirits, speaking in tongues and more.

"Everyone has gifts. Being a student, mother, or father is a gift. With all these gifts comes balance. If all were healers, who would teach knowledge? If all were miracle workers, who would raise the children? You are all a part of the One, each no less than the other.

"One of the difficulties of the community lies not in believing that healers exist but in the knowledge that some healers exploit their gifts. They believe, therefore, that all healers exploit their gifts. The gift may be genuine, but some healers forget to remember from whence the gift came.

"When healers become so puffed-up with importance, and give credit to their own self, and become noisy with boasting about healing successes and charge exorbitant fees, then they are exploiting their gift. They are as noisy clangs and only that.

"Woe to any person giving false pretense when it comes to being a messenger of God in any way."

"On one assignment, I worked in coma recovery and, on another, I worked with neonates. Some people question how an unconscious person or an infant can receive healing if they cannot express faith."

Jesus interrupted me at this point to say, *"All it takes is a simple thought or prayer with an intent to heal. Then, by letting go and letting God, you allow God to take over. You are born realizing an innate oneness in God. Infants are aware from whence they came and, in that subconscious remembering, have simply natural faith and trust in God. Coma patients can often hear and be guided during healing and recovery. And, if they can't hear, they, too, remember from within."*

"That brings to mind something that happened several years ago. My brother-in-law was in a coma in the hospital. He and his wife had been very skeptical of my healing gift, but were kind enough not to say anything. When his wife was at the hospital, I visited her, not to offer healing for her husband, but to support her in her time of trial. The first visit, I simply was with her in the waiting room. The next day, I went back, and she was in the intensive care unit with her husband. I joined her and we spent time talking while her husband lay in bed. Suddenly I was moved to say to her, 'I do Healing Touch.' Immediately, she excitedly said, 'Oh, would you, would you, please!' And so, I went up to the bed to scan her husband's aura. In the meantime, his daughter, my niece, came in, and while we were all standing alongside of the bed, the doctor came in.

"This doctor knew of my healing gift. He knew I had

been in the emergency room and elsewhere in the hospital doing healing work when called upon. He stood alongside of the wife and told her that her husband was dying, partly because he was unable to get enough oxygen into his lungs. He explained why nothing more could be done. When he left, I looked down at my brother-in-law lying in bed, and for some wonderful reason, I felt moved to suddenly drop my hands over his lungs and push down with force, shouting out loud, 'Bill, did you hear that?! You are going to die if you don't start breathing from down here!' As I pushed even harder on his lungs, again I shouted, even louder, 'Did you hear that?!' He came out of his coma, opened his eyes, and winked at me!

"Even in a coma, he had heard my message, strong and clear. He went home within a few weeks, and tended a garden the next spring. He has outlived his wife."

"Skeptics only see what they perceive as unsuccessful healings, not realizing all the underlying factors that make up why a person was healed or not, or even what is healed. Healing does not have to mean that a miraculous change in physical condition occurs. You are made up of so much more than the physical. You are a spiritual being, an emotional being, a mindful being, and a physical being. Healing involves every aspect of your life. You all have the capacity for facilitating healing. You do it all of the time without realizing it."

"I have often told people that healing is not something you do only when you are sick. It is a part of the process and journey of life. Healing embraces every aspect of your life."

"However, listen when I tell you, everyone is capable of healing self and others. You heal others when you listen to, pray for, love, comfort and hug a grieving friend, say kind words to others, or even when you pat someone on the back. Often it is simply making someone feel well enough to cope with the stresses in their lives, not always a physical healing. This is all a part of the healing process."

"Wouldn't God's love be enough to give me what I need to be healthy of body, mind, and spirit?"

"Love must be continually given and received to generate healthy energy. For much of mankind, God's love is overshadowed and darkened by feelings of unworthiness or doubt. This unworthiness and doubt and feelings of not being loved lead to destructive thoughts, habits and addictions of all kinds, resulting in poor health of body, mind and spirit. With your free will, the choice is yours to accept or refuse God's love. If you truly accept God's love, you automatically generate love toward self and others and, in turn, strive to become healthier in all aspects of your life."

"Why, then, would a person be physically, mentally, or spiritually handicapped if they are loved?"

"Even though feelings of not being loved or even an inability to give love may result in poor health, an unhealthy person might very well be loved and capable of loving. You must remember there is more to a person than the body. There may be karmic reasons for ill health. However physical or mental handicaps do not necessarily relate to a person's past sins. Through free will, some souls may lovingly

choose to carry another person's burden, and other souls may have deliberately chosen afflictions in order to learn some needed lesson of compassion or tolerance.

"There is a special place in the heart of God for the infirmed. Again I say, God so loved the world that He gave His only begotten Son, that whosoever believeth in Him shall not perish but shall have everlasting life. It is as simple as that. The infirmed will experience surrender, by letting go and letting God take care of them, far sooner than the young and fit. They live in the presence of and in the hands of God. Would that all humans could come to that state of belief. Therein would the world be a better place to live."

"I went through a period when nothing seemed to be happening with healing of anyone. One day, when I was greatly discouraged, I prayed for answers, wondering if this was the end of my healing gift, or if I was doing something wrong. I called the local pastor, who was a friend, and he didn't answer me; he just listened. I called my new healer friend and she didn't answer me; she just listened. The next day, at work, the first hand patient said, 'Since you have been doing this, I don't have pain any more.' The second patient came in and said, 'Since you have been doing this, I sleep nights now.' The third patient came in and said, 'Since you have been doing this, I am coping so much better with my pain. I can live with this now.'

"God was, once again, teaching me a lesson. I realized then that healing is not always a physical change. Sometimes it is relief of pain, but not necessarily cure. Sometimes it is an increased ability to have a restful sleep to tolerate the pain of tomorrow. Sometimes it is emotional healings or spiritual healings.

"When I received my healing gift, I . . ."

Interrupting me, Jesus said, "*You did not just recently receive a healing gift. It has been a part of you for many lifetimes. You, simply, finally remembered in this lifetime. What you did receive was help in remembering.*"

"It would be interesting to know of all of those lifetimes, and yet, I truly feel my present lifetime is what I need to focus on right now.

"In every community across the nation where I went to work, I found a gym and a church. Amazingly, the pastors were very open to my gift and supported me beautifully, often leading me to people needing healing. Healings happened, and yet, I felt that it should not generally be made known that I was a healer. Only when I felt a need to do so, did I speak of my gift.

"When I would go to my home town between traveling assignments, I often ran into skepticism. I had written to my pastor back home and Father John, a family priest, of all that was taking place. They appeared to accept and be interested in the healings.

"One evening, when I was home between assignments, a daughter and I went to visit Father John. He was entertaining a guest and they were about to sit down for dinner. They invited us to join them. We declined the food but did sit and talk with them. Father John's guest asked me, 'What do you do for a living?' I answered him, 'I am a traveling occupational therapist.' Father John interrupted me before I could go on and emphatically said, 'No! Tell him what you really do!' Then began a very lively conversation about healing, with the two of them joining in and prodding me on, and my daughter smiling at my side.

"Another time when I was home between assignments, I went to the Lutheran church I grew up in, for an adult Sunday school class. I had no idea what the Bible study was going to be about.

"My pastor announced to the class, 'We have a healer in our midst.' Everyone looked around and an old friend of mine turned to me and said, 'It's you, isn't it?' I was not comfortable. I knew many people were skeptical and I did not want to make waves. However my pastor said to me, 'Tell them about. . . .' And then, 'Tell them about. . . .' I had written to him about many healings and, as soon as I finished telling about one, he would urge me into telling them about another.

"Near the end of the class, he read a passage from the Bible pertaining to the day's lesson. He read from Mark, the sixth chapter: 'And Jesus said to them, a prophet is not without honor, except in his own country, and among his own kin, and in his own house. And he could do no mighty work there, except that he laid his hands upon a few sick people and healed them. And he marveled because of their unbelief.'"

"Ah, Saint Ta, do not waste time grieving over loss of church family and friends because of their lack of faith in you. You were led to Song of the Morning, where you are accepted with honor and without question and where you can fulfill your life's work. Oh, Brave Heart! Know you are

being upheld in the eyes of the Lord.

"It will come to pass that healers will work side-by-side with clergy, doctors and nurses, all the time, everywhere. It is happening already. It is not an accident. Many clergy, doctors and nurses are themselves healers. Your efforts and healings in the hospitals and nursing homes were not in vain. You have helped to lay a foundation, along with many other healers. Communities need the medical approach and the healers, working together.

"Presently, in the medical field, discoveries in medicine are not enough to assist mankind with advancing bacteria, for which there are few known antibiotics. Healers can help enhance the effects of antibiotics and hasten healing.

"Stress, anxiety, grief and loss of spirit trigger hormones that suppress resistance to disease and have a direct influence on health. Mankind covers up these feelings with drugs to make it go away, without really getting to the bottom of the problem. Healers can help alleviate or eliminate stresses through listening, prayer, laying on of hands and creative visualization.

"Mankind would have fewer serious illnesses if they could be more open with their feelings as events happen or are felt, and set their mind on continuing their life in the presence of God—in love and health. Not everyone develops an illness as a result of tragedy or loss. It depends on how they cope with their problems.

"Keep in mind that God did have a hand in creating drugs. People with imbalances of body chemicals, diabetes, heart conditions, cancer and many other disabilities rely on drugs to heal, prolong and improve their lives."

"You sound like me. All that you said sounds like something I have been telling others for a long time."

"What you have taught is truth from within you, Saint Ta. As you set your mind on God, God guided you daily to access and teach these truths."

"Sometimes when I teach a class, I wonder about the varying levels of spiritual development of the people attending. I start with a prayer familiar to me, 'May the words of my mouth and the meditations of my heart be acceptable to you, oh God.' Then I generally say, 'If you are able to remember even one thing I say to you that enhances your ability to live in the presence of God, in that remembrance, realize . . . that God intervened in your life today.'"

"You and others have taken my yoke upon yourself and have learned from me. Teach others as I have taught you."

"Things have changed for me. In the presence of God, when I teach, words just come from within."

"You are a great teacher."

"I wouldn't say 'great.' "

"I would. Tell everyone what you teach and let them decide."

"Well, for one thing . . . I feel it is important that we, daily, clear the aura of negative energies before they manifest on the body as ill health. This is a powerful, preventive measure. It is something you should do every day, like brushing your teeth. A habit. I simply reach out and, prayerfully, very slowly, sweep the aura smooth wherever I am; or, if I am in the shower, I use a mental affirmation, imagining the water cleansing my aura; or I sit on a stool, put on soft music, and meditatively clear the aura surrounding my body by 'dancing with the spirits.' I feel so much better when I do this. This helps to prevent physical illness before it even occurs."

"Healing is part of the process and journey of life. If you think of the whole person, you will soon realize you are not just a physical being. Healing embraces every aspect of you."

"I also teach centering oneself and increasing awareness of spiritual guides for healing. Further I teach setting aside the ego during healing, demanding it take leave, to eliminate distracting thoughts and desires. Self-interest interferes with healing. Without the ego there is only love.

"I teach people how to heal themselves and then to go on to heal others. I also teach about the chakra system from the standpoint of physical, mental and spiritual expression, as healing embraces every aspect of one's life."

"I said that before."

"What did you say before?"

"That healing embraces every aspect of your life."

"Pretty funny, are we mirroring each other now?"

"When you are so connected to the One, you, even as unique individuals, do mirror each other in loving action and thoughts."

"Like husband and wife?"

"Yes, in spiritual communion."

* * *

I worked in many different settings: skilled nursing centers, outpatient therapy, hand clinics, neonatal, intensive care, cardiac units, rehabilitation clinics. When asked what I was doing, as I moved my hands over a person for healing, I often would say, "Healing Touch," even though I had not started to study. Healing Touch seemed to be a modality sometimes accepted in the medical community. Also, I soon learned to get prior approval, to do healing work, from either the administration or the department head when starting a new assignment, and then from any patient I might work with. Occasionally, I had an opportunity to educate staff about healing, and often staff members approached me for personal healing.

I was sent to Alpena, Michigan for an occupational therapy assignment. I concluded, before going there, that they would not understand my healing gift, and therefore I chose not to use it. I got away with that for about two weeks, when one fine day I heard someone screaming from down the hall. Without hesitation, I left the therapy room and followed the screams to where I found two nurse aides simply trying to help a resident transfer out of her wheelchair. Without hesitation, I said to the nurse aides, "I have a method for calming people. Can I use it?" They both immediately agreed that anything would be better than this upset woman. So I put one hand just off the top of her head and slowly brought it down, and off, the front of her body. She took a deep sigh and melted into a relaxed state.

The nurse aides were so taken back by what happened

that, after I left, they went to the director of nursing and, in turn, the administrator. I was called into the director's office. They questioned, "What are you doing to our residents?" At the time I was not studying anything about healing, but I knew that my healer friend in New Mexico who taught me to 'let go and let God' was a teacher of Healing Touch. I was moved to say to the director and the administrator, "It is Healing Touch, taught in some nursing curricula." They asked, "Can you get us some statistics?" "I don't think so," I answered, "but I can get you some information." They settled for that. After work, I called my healer friend, and she sent me information on Healing Touch.

In the meantime, I was angry with the nurse aides for having got me into this situation. That night I thought about how I might feel toward the nurse aides when I would see them the next day. I prayed for help for dealing with the nurse aides and the whole situation. God spoke to me . . . "Whatever you do, do it with love."

The next day, I saw the nurse aides and felt nothing but love for them, and before I could even say anything to them, they were apologizing. I took the Healing Touch information into the office, and they studied it for a day, then called me, once again, into a meeting.

"We have decided that you can use this. We would like you to start with Mrs. . . . and Mr. . . . for now. We are sure they could benefit from this." Hesitantly I said, "It doesn't work that way for me. I never know why I am moved to heal one person or another. It is God's will—a nudge, urge, push, shove—calling me toward them. I can try, but it may not be successful."

"Well then, if you are going to be waving your hands over residents here, we feel you should have an inservice so staff will know what to expect." I agreed, and the class was very well attended.

While I was still in that same facility, a nurse came to me and told me a doctor wanted to talk to me in a patient's room. He was standing on the far side of the patient's bed. As I approached him he asked, "Would you scan her body and tell me what you find?" This was interesting, first of all, that a doctor would use this terminology, and secondly, ask for my participation. I told him, "I can scan her body and tell you where her problem lies, but I may not be able to tell you what the problem is." He replied, "I'll settle for that."

This very elderly patient had had a broken hip, resulting in much pain. Nursing staff had been positioning her on her good hip to relieve the pain. I scanned her body and found a problem in her good hip, so I said to the doctor, "I would suggest getting an x-ray for her other hip. I think that hip is also broken." He did get the x-ray, and she did have a second broken hip.

Ever present, Jesus said, *"And now you have a healing room at home."*

"Ah, yes, Sweet Jesus, my healing room is wonderful, but I can't help but remember that, in the hospitals and nursing homes, there simply is no healing room and I can't spend a lot of time on a patient.

"In professional settings such as these, I feel as if I am

two different persons yet one. I am working as an occupational therapist, and I am also in the presence of God in a prayerful, meditative state. In this meditative state of awareness, all things are possible. I scan a person's body or lay my hands on someone, knowing that, if it is God's will, the person will be healed in some way. As a therapist, it is appropriate for me to lay my hands on someone while I work with them, but not always appropriate for clergy or others to do so. I did healing in this way in so many instances I cannot even count them.

"One time, in a setting where healers were not allowed to work, I had a patient that could not turn her head, even slightly, from one side to the other. As I was standing behind her wheelchair, I simply put my hands on her shoulders and, while talking to a physical therapist, I also brought my awareness to God and, instantly, became fully conscious of the fact that she was being healed of this affliction. There was no outward sign of what was taking place. I said nothing. The next day, when she came in for therapy, she told me that, since I had put my hands on her shoulders, she could now turn her head left and right and demonstrated it. Also, she was fully aware of what had taken place.

"Now that I am semi-retired and do not have much access to hospitals, I use my healing room at home. I continue to work in the presence of God while using prayer, meditation, intuition, soft music, warmth, incense, and healing visualizations, most often with color. Relaxation and healing are enhanced by all or combinations of these different methods."

"Feel good therapy."

Laughing I said, "A doctor I once worked with, who was very skeptical, sarcastically called spiritual healing, 'feel good therapy.' I replied so fast that I don't think the words were mine, 'So what's wrong with feeling good.' That caught his attention and got him thinking."

"All who work in the medical and healing professions are making people 'feel good.' It is all 'feel good therapy.'"

"In my healing room during relaxing feel good therapy, healing happens more often than you would imagine. It is God's healing grace that does the healing and none other. And it can happen in an instant.

"Often, I am aware that healing is occurring during counseling with someone simply wanting to talk about their problems. Sometimes as I work with one person out of a group, I realize that healing is occurring in another person in the same room at the same time."

"Anyone who enters your healing room receives a blessing."

"One time, I simply put my hands on a man's stomach as he lay on my healing table. I left my hands there for a long time as he ranted and raved about all the problems in his life. On and on he went, emphatically telling me all that was bothering him. Still I left my hands there. Suddenly, in mid-sentence, he stopped, deeply sighed, and said, 'Wow! I really needed this.' He was silent after that, in deep relaxation, and my hands rested on him for a long time before

Spirit moved them.

"I found when I do 'laying on of hands,' I am not in control of my hands. I wait for my hands to move off the person. They simply lift off without any thought from me of doing this. Sometimes it happens after only a short time, and often it takes much longer. My hands meld into the person as if they had become a part of that person. Other times I am visualizing organs or other body parts while healing is occurring.

"Often, when I heal someone, I pray: 'May the words of my mouth and the meditations of my heart be acceptable to You, oh God.' Upon saying these words, I turn it over to God.

"Oh, Sweet Jesus, here I am, writing of this beautiful communication with you. Sometimes I worry that I am letting too much of me slip in. Am I giving false testimony in any way?"

"There should be no doubt in your mind that what you share is truth. You are strength and delicacy and, in your asking, you shall receive notice when it is not acceptable. Your writings are given many blessings."

I felt a heavy weight upon myself momentarily. It bordered on grief. How could I be so blissful one moment and grieved the next? What was happening to me? I said, "Jesus, I feel a heavy heart at this moment. I need to get past it. Can you help me, Sweet Jesus?"

"Your heavy heart is not from what you think. There are many negative actions taking place in the world today and some of it is surfacing in you in this moment. Brave Heart,

be strong. Go within . . . meditate . . . send love unto the world."

> I cry silent tears
> with each breath I take.
> Heaviness surrounds me.
> "Lift my spirit,
> God of gentleness."

I stopped what I was doing and curled up in my big, purple easy chair. I laid my head on the arm of the chair and totally relaxed. I meditated no more than five minutes, sending love to the world everywhere. In that five minutes, I saw war-torn cities, villages and countrysides, laid to waste. I saw government spending money on weapons instead of restructuring cities. I saw greed, hunger, poverty, homelessness, hopelessness. What children I did see were armed. I also saw strength in convictions and anti-Americanism. I saw families torn apart. I could only send love. That was all I could do.

"Love is important, Saint Ta, especially now. People are truly afraid, and what they are afraid of, they attract. Fears must be dispelled."

"Sweet Jesus, people talk to me in desperation." I said this because, again, I was seeing a vision . . . of many people coming forth with their overwhelming needs, their anguish held within in quiet desperation, then releasing it all out to me—exclaiming . . . questioning . . . expressing pain, sorrow, fears and unhappiness:

Oh Lord, why am I so desperate? Why is there this

need all the time? Where are you, Lord? Why aren't you more present in my life? Why do we have to struggle so? Why is there war? Why can't I feel more from you? Where is my spiritual life anyway? I can't find it any more. Is it only present when things are going well and we are grateful? What is there for me to be grateful for? I plead, and you don't hear. I scream inwardly, and you don't notice. I am here, Lord, help me. Where are you? I feel abandoned. I feel like there is no hope. I'm hungry and thirsty. I hurt. I just don't believe any more. I have all these needs, and you don't pay any attention. I have nothing to be thankful for any more. I have no will; I haven't had it for a long time.

* * *

In their desperation, I felt their overwhelming hopelessness. I had heard all of this and more over my years as a healer and counselor, and yet, now it seemed it was all coming back in one big united voice, as if all desperation came from one longing.

"In their desperation and in their asking, there is doubt in God. If they doubt, there is no room for believing, and in their doubting, they need to hear the answers over and over again. That is one reason why you are writing these books—to help remove doubts by teaching them that God loves them no matter what they do. If they believe, there will be no room for doubt. When they learn to give all to God, they will feel God's ever-present love, and fears will diminish. Often they assume they are not loved. Love is

eternal; it is within all creation.

"Saint Ta, you and others have borne their burdens and given them love and light. That is all that is required of you."

"Sweet Jesus, they need so much more than love. These are desperate people. How is God going to put food into their mouths and tend their wounds?"

"All people are karmically involved in their lives. Love is action. Living in love will attract goodness, and needs will be met and karma removed. Love will lead people to help each other. For those less fortunate who do not receive help, they may, necessarily, need to experience the present situation to fulfill karma. Still, they too can learn to live in love.

"Ah Brave Heart, your unconditional love serves you well. You have done well in bearing the burdens of others and then giving them up to God."

And with that, I did let it all go—the vision, the desperation and the burdens. Layers upon layers of burdens flowed from me as I gave it all to God. Joy filled me and I felt blessed rest.

* * *

I asked Jesus what so many others have asked of me, "How can we recognize a true healer?"

"A true healer merges readily with God's healing grace in meditation, prayer and faith while addressing sickness of mind, body, or spirit in others. A true healer lives in the presence of God, and comfortably opens to and welcomes

interaction with God. None of this can be achieved through ego."

"I have heard some miracle workers, including healers, use spiritual power for selfish purposes."

"As I said before of the false master, the same goes for false Christs, false miracle workers, false prophets and others. They may show great miracles and wonders yet have inflated, egotistical charisma that charms, entrances and deceives even the greatest of you. They may convince you they are teaching true righteousness, and yet they will be unable to reflect the loving presence of God at all times to others. They will not be truth. Be wary of these false deceivers.

"It may appear that they benefit from their deceptions, but that will only be temporary. Lo, I tell you, no act of unkindness will go unnoticed. For what you sow, you reap."

"It would seem difficult to trust anyone."

"Use your intuition. Your own truth will not allow you to choose falsely. True healers and teachers will empower you to remain true unto thine own self. You will recognize them by their unconditional love.

"If all the world were to sit idly by, in distrust of each other, who would address law, justice, healing and mercy? Nothing would get done. Truth is action, just as love is action. Even the simplest act of love holds within it a miracle of healing."

"Some years back, one of my granddaughters came over to stay with me one evening. I had just finished a rough day at work and she realized I was stressed. She said to me, 'I want to give you a healing treatment, Grandma.' She looked at me and said, 'Are you ticklish?' She knew better. One touch from her and we were rolling around on the floor, laughing hysterically. What a wonderful healing treatment!

"Other times, she has scanned her mother's body to determine how her mother was feeling. She has been known to say, 'There is nothing wrong with you, Mom,' or 'You have a headache, Mom.'"

"She will continue to blossom like a rose."

"Her middle name is Rose."

"We know."

"Sometimes, in my healing work with clients, I feel as if my whole self is being filled up with energized air, and a soft exhalation comes from within me, without prompting. As the air flows out, the exhaling lasts so much longer than when I inhale. Often I am moved to blow gently on a client, resulting in relaxation, decreased pain, or a healing. At first, I didn't know why this was happening. Here I was, sometimes blowing on my patients' hands in hand therapy, and I didn't know why. I remember, like all mothers, I would gently blow on my children's little injuries. Even now, I sometimes blow on my own injuries, an innate, immediate reaction to a burn or cut. In my healing work, I intuitively feel it as the breath of God."

"It is."

"I know, and yet other times, I feel so filled up, I am

moved to forcefully blow the breath away from the client and myself."

"When this happens, you are instantly taking on their problems or karma and then releasing them. It can only be done with unconditional love, and since you have no hold on their problems or their karma, you simply send them to God through breath. It happens naturally for you."

I was taken back by what He said. I know taking on others' karma is serious business, yet I often wondered if that was what I was doing with the breath.

As I mentioned briefly in *Sustained by Faith*, after two years of not reading anything about healing and going only with the natural lessons from God as teacher, I was finally, strongly moved to study different methods of healing. I could not ignore the sudden urgency of the message. I had prided myself on receiving everything I needed for healing from Spirit. And suddenly, without warning, I was given this emphatic message to start studying. It was one of those messages that you just can't ignore, because if you do, you feel totally discombobulated. So I started taking all the classes I could, on all aspects of healing.

I was living in New Mexico and the first class I took was "Holoenergetics," through the Upledger Institute. Looking back, I realize this was the perfect class for me to be taking when just starting out. Healing with love was the emphasis, and what could be more basic in healing than love? It was open to the public and taught simplistically.

I learned how loving energy can improve the quality and taste of what we eat. As I mentioned before, we were instructed to send loving energy into a flask of water, while another flask of water was ignored. It was amazing how much sweeter the energized water was, compared to the ignored water. For me, this was proof that love and energy work can alter and heal.

Then a Lutheran pastor recommended classes on aura balancing. One of the people who attended the classes was an eighty-five year old kinesiologist. He was able to tell, by muscle testing, where healing was needed. During the classes, he was unable to feel the aura, much like some of you. He wanted so much to be able to do so. The classes lasted three days just for the first level, a total of twenty-four hours. On the last day, the kinesiologist suddenly felt the aura. He was so excited he could hardly contain himself. Sometimes it takes even longer to be able to feel this subtle energy. But it is possible. In these classes I learned that I could use a pendulum as a tool to quickly locate and dispel entities (invading, possessing, or influencing spirits) and determine the state of the chakras and condition of the physical and subtle bodies, even though I intuitively already knew how to do this without the pendulum.

I attended Healing Touch classes in Albuquerque, New Mexico. These classes originated in nursing curricula across the nation. Now it is taught to anyone. Each level is a three-day weekend. There are three levels, with sublevels and additional classes on spiritual ministry. Healing Touch is being increasingly recognized by the medical profession because of its scientific and intellectual presentation of the art of healing.

I attended Cranio-Sacral Therapy classes taught through

the Upledger Institute and also by a presenter who offered it here at Song of the Morning Retreat. It involves a subtle physiological rhythm within the semi-closed hydraulic system that envelopes the brain and spinal cord. An intuitive skill is needed to sense this rhythm and the therapeutic pulses.

I attended many classes and group sessions of Reiki, another healing modality.

I feel blessed to have been made aware of my natural healing gift prior to reading or studying. Taking classes in many aspects of the healing arts has not drastically changed what I do. I now know terminology and certain techniques. Even so, healing basically depends on faith, unconditional love, and divine guidance, through God's grace.

"You don't need to study any more. You never did. You were urged to do so to come to that realization. You will remember even more and learn from the doing. You will never stop remembering and learning. So, as in the beginning when we urged you not to study, I again urge you not to study. There is no need to study. Spirit will help you remember what you already know. Read only for pleasure."

"I feel your love, Saint Ta. I feel your love, and it fills up the universes for all eternity. Your faith and love is what heals. God is love."

As I listened to Jesus talking, I was feeling such a blissful sense of peace and love. I realized that little had changed, from the beginning of my awareness of my healing gift to this moment in my life with all the classes behind me. What I discovered is amazing. The healing methods I studied and my initial gift are more alike than different. Another lesson learned.

There are endless varieties of modalities used by healers, each healer eventually settling on what is appropriate for their work. After all the classes, I continue to use my intuition to guide me, often incorporating a combination of modalities. There is no regret in having taken the classes.

"Stay open to new, ongoing revelations."

"Oh, I know. It seems that, every time I think there is nothing more to learn, something happens and a new discovery emerges, seemingly through desire and a willingness for Spirit to lead me.

"When His Holiness Cealo, a Buddhist monk, came to visit, he told me to simply heal souls. He did not give me directions at that moment nor did I ask for any. However, that evening, a woman came to me in spirit form. I knew she wanted her soul healed. I didn't know what to do. I saw her soul as brilliant light and deep darkness. I thought maybe I should remove the dark, and yet, I hesitated and did nothing. She soon disappeared. The next morning at the breakfast table, in front of all present, I told Cealo about the night visitor and my experience of thinking I should remove the dark. He adamantly said, 'Oh no, never take away the dark; the person would die. Increase the light!'"

"There is ever-new rejoicing when someone is attuned to the spirit world. In your attunement there is amazing faith, strength and trust. The more you open, the more rejoicing and communion happens between you and Spirit."

"Ah, Sweet Jesus, I am blessed to have all of you in my life. Thank you for your love."

* * *

"Functioning on earth as a human is difficult at times. I sometimes wonder if God really knows what it is like to be in a human body. I see so much suffering and I experience arthritic pain."

"Some sources say God sent me, so that God could experience what humankind is suffering, through me. That is not so. He already knows of your pain."

"Tell me, Sweet Jesus, Why did God create pain? "

"God did not create pain or suffering. God created your physical body, with a sensory system to alert you of bodily injury, ill health and outside influences, for your own physical safety and health.

"Even more so, the original intent for the sensory system was to provide you experiences of God in the beauty, life, and the intelligence of nature as one.

"Then mankind began to be influenced by dualities within the earth plane and, instead of remembering the oneness of pain, pleasure, joy and all there is, mankind accepted pain and suffering as separate. This inability to be at one with all aspects of creation led to a perceived separation from, and diminished ability to commune with, The Divine. And the chasm grew ever wider.

"That is why, Saint Ta, your books and others are being written, to remind everyone that heaven is within, lying in wait to be acknowledged through the realization that all is

one in Christ Consciousness.

"Within creation's duality all humans, including heal-ers, experience pain—physical, emotional and spiritual. Still, you do not have to suffer anguish with it, nor dwell upon it. It is said that even I, upon earth, suffered. Yes, I suffered greatly within the physical earth experience, and too, I grieved for mankind. Still, I knew, in harmonious oneness was my pain, suffering, and my joy.

"Those who feel, face and share the pains and sufferings of each other and of the world, within the consciousness of oneness, are in close communion with the very essence of their lives and have found God within. They are embracing the experience and harmonizing with it. In that harmonious embracing, with countless expressions of unconditional love, they learn, grow and experience heaven on earth as one.

"I have said before, 'Bear one another's burdens.' Many have chosen to bear the burdens of the healed in their healing. Much of what you feel, Saint Ta, is others' pain that you willingly take on. In that pain lies your strength. If you did not have the ability to continually real-ize pain as a part of the One, you would not be in this world today."

"I have seen you in the faces of patients, children and aged, and yes, I see the harmony of suffering and joy in them and in myself. Thank you for the remembrances, Sweet Jesus, and for all you do for us."

"Bless you, Saint Ta. Keep God consciousness always uppermost in your mind, not pain consciousness. Walk al-

ways in the presence of God. Your pain is not all your own. Let it go . . . into the oneness. Lose body consciousness every chance you can, and the Father will give you rest."

I stopped here, thinking about my pain, which comes and goes. Instead of letting these thoughts go, I felt myself tensing and bringing the pain on. I couldn't let it go. It built to a painful crescendo as I clenched my fists and all of my body. All of my pain was gathered together into one bundle. Approaching a point of unbearable pain, I suddenly was moved to consciously embrace it. I entered it and became the pain. Almost immediately, a wave of relief flowed through me and washed it away. It was as if I had canceled the pain.

Then in the back of my mind, there was a little message that said, "I wonder if it is gone forever or just for now." There was that doubt again. "What is wrong with me that I have such doubt? How am I to rid myself of pain consciousness forever?"

Ever present, Jesus entered my questioning and said, *"Thinking about your pain is keeping it in your consciousness. Do not suffer with it."*

I was reminded of the pain I experienced while in therapy after my awakening. I had excruciating pain in my legs every time I would walk on the treadmill, and I could not go much farther than a quarter mile, at a very slow pace. One day I decided to meditate while walking. I gathered my pain into one extremely painful bundle and merged into it. This canceled the pain. Continuing my meditation, I was able to walk well over a mile before someone stopped me.

My heart rate had not increased at all!

Now, I realized that, in gathering my pain while tensing my body, I had just experienced the same thing. Bundling up the pain and embracing it works. Pain is also gone when I can become so one with God that I lose body consciousness. Then there is nothing bothering me at all.

Continuing on in heart talk with Jesus, "While alone, I found that creative visualization and deep meditation helped me relax and heal. I found also that I was able to lead others in creative visualizations to help them relax and heal. I want to put one in here, at this time, if that is okay with you."

"Sounds like a fine idea. Can I play, too?"

Laughing, I invited Him in.

"One should make this time as comfortable and beautiful as possible. Even though I like to 'set the stage' with candles and so forth, you may wish to do a visualization without any prior preparation, for instance, while in bed trying to fall asleep or when a certain area of your body is in pain.

"If you like, put on relaxing, peaceful music, light a candle or many candles and burn some incense. Lie down or sit in a comfortable position. If you are in pain, it will be difficult to focus on the visualization, so try to be as comfortable as you can. Sometimes I like to put a blanket in the dryer to get it nice and warm and then wrap up in it.

"Now, I want you to stop, pause and collect yourself . . . relax into yourself. . . .

Mentally, acknowledge God with a prayer of praise and

thanksgiving. . . . Say an intention for what you desire, or ask for nothing. . . . Keep your mind on your breathing as you breathe naturally, in and out. . . . Focus on your breath.

Imagine that with each inhalation you are taking in God's love. . . . Fill your heart with this love. . . . Breathe in love. Breathe out love. . . . Think only on your breath . . . as love.

After a while, imagine your heart expanding and contracting as you breathe in and out. . . .

Now, imagine your breath becomes a soft, pink color.

Breathe in the pink color. . . . Let it radiate throughout your body. . . . You become this soft, pink color, pure and unblemished love. . . .

Keep breathing, in . . . and out. . . . A pure pink color, ever expanding . . . radiating into your body. . . . If your breathing slows down, let it do so. . . .

Fill yourself with the warmth of love. . . .

Cancel all other thoughts. . . . Erase them. . . . Concentrate only on your breathing.

Now, as you breathe in, hold your breath. . . .

Feel the warm, pink breath radiate throughout your body quickly . . . as you slowly release the breath.

Again, breathe in. . . . Hold your breath as you direct the warmth into any area in your body that needs healing, or it may lead you to a different area. Follow it.

Slowly breathe the suffering out. . . .

Breathe in . . . hold your breath . . . paint it pink. . . .
Feel the warmth spread. . . . Imagine your breath is
quickly traveling inside your body . . . right to where it
should go.

Hold it in that area for just a second . . . release. Again,
breathe in, and slowly out through the painful area. . . .
Imagine the warm breath taking the pain out, replacing
it with love. . . .

Let your breath work for you. . . . Do this over and
over, breathing in through the nose, letting it radiate
down and slowly out a painful area . . . over and over.

When your intuition tells you to stop, slowly come back
to ordinary consciousness."

* * *

"That was wonderful, I enjoyed that!"

He was radiating pink colors!

"Sweet Jesus, some people tell me they cannot visualize
anything."

*"I tell you, everyone can visualize. If you can visualize
food set before you, you can visualize anything. Visualizing
is beneficial for your health and peace of mind. Some call it
day-dreaming, which is an innate means for relieving stress
and increasing relaxation. There is a time and a place for
day-dreaming or visualizing. Work, school, driving and
other times that require your focused attention are not
good times for drifting off. Before falling asleep, intention-*

ally visualizing the good and beautiful brings about healing and pleasant dreams.

"Creative visualization will help you to increase your self-realization and reawaken the creative child within you even more. You will begin to become more aware of your oneness with the world around you and with God."

"Thank you, Sweet Jesus. Many times I have been comforted by a pink angel who I imagined wrapping me in her wings and holding me close. Often I have left her with others to give comfort. Children in the hospitals love my pink angel. No one has ever refused the loan of my pink angel. And there have been many times when, as a child and even as an adult, I have imagined crawling up on your lap for comfort."

"And in your imaginings, I held you close."

"I love you, Sweet Jesus."

Chapter Seven

Reincarnation

"but I tell you that Elijah has already come,
and they did not know him,
but did to him whatever they pleased. . . ."
Then the disciples understood
that he was speaking to them of
John the Baptist.

—Matthew (17:12-13)

"I have a strong Christian background. I have always been told that we have only one life. It even says that in the Bible somewhere."

"To all I say . . . truly that is a misinterpretation. You have one soul but many spirits. Therein is the one life: in the soul. Each incarnation is a new spirit of the one soul. Each lifetime increasingly allows spiritual growth, which strengthens the soul. Eventually your soul will not have any further desires or karma and will be content within the realization that the presence of God is enough. Then and then only will you go to be with God. Yet, even then, you are free

to choose reincarnation to aid humanity.

"The concept of reincarnation is not new. It was written of in biblical books and passages. They were removed or rewritten when Church fathers decided man became too lax with so many lifetimes available for him to reach final liberation."

"I am amazed that Church fathers could suddenly change the mind-set of so many people. Didn't people question this?"

"This happened during a time in history in which one did not ask questions. They had the fear of God, hell and damnation infused within their hearts, given by Church authority. In some cases, this is true even in your present time."

"That is strong language."

"I am a rebel at heart."

"Ah, my Sweet Jesus a rebel?"

"You always say, 'It's the squeaky wheel that gets the grease.'"

Trying to contain my laughter I continued, "Is there anything written about karma and reincarnation in the remaining Bible passages?"

"You can still find passages in the Bible about karma and reincarnation if you are able to truly understand what is written. I am pleased that this is being addressed in many aspects of life in this new age. Finally liberation will be more fully understood."

"And now You use the term 'New Age,' which represents a group of what many consider rebellious New Agers."

"It is human nature to fear change— fear of losing group or self-identity-egoism; fear of having to learn something new-ego. It is only in change that growth happens."

"Is sin the same thing as karma?"

"Sin is the human conception of the action and the result of wrongdoing. Karma is what you receive as a result of good or sinful action. What you sow, you reap. As I said before, if you are good, goodness follows. If you sin and do not truly forgive yourself and others, you receive like karmic reward.

"Woe to the person that takes upon himself or herself the responsibility of judging another person and delving out punishment, outside of the greater law of God and of the land. That person will be equally guilty of the sin."

"How can the result of sinning be considered a karmic reward?"

"Think of a reward as compensation for your actions. If you do wrong, your reward will come back to you in some way similar to what you did wrong. You are always given the choice to experience these same lessons over and over again until you finally learn to forgive yourself and others, sin no more, and live in love. If you are loving, you will receive only good in return.

"If it seems to you as if you are able to do wrong and are not being punished for it, you are only fooling yourself.

"Listen when I tell you . . . playing at life in wrongful doing does not come anywhere near to the excitement and bliss one experiences when living in joy and love and watching those circumstances play out.

"With free will, some souls may have deliberately chosen to return with afflictions in order to learn some needed lesson of humility, tolerance, or compassion. Even babies that die young may have returned in order to help the parents develop understanding through such loss. So therefore, physical illness may be of importance in their existence. Still, not all misfortunes relate to past misdeeds of self. Some are meant for future experiences for yourself and for others. That is why healers must be alert and realize the difference between those who can be healed as opposed to those who are not to be healed."

"I often wondered why I am drawn to heal some people and not others. It is an inner-knowing.

"Do we ever get rid of bad karma?"

"I was sent to earth to free mankind of all past sins. At the time of my death, all past karmic debt was forgiven . . . forgotten. All could start fresh. Through all that I say, have said, and do, many souls were, are, and will be saved by their belief. However, there are many who did not listen then and still, today, do not listen. People need to pay attention and hear this message over and over. By living in love and non-judgment, forgiving yourself and all others, and sinning no more, you can rise above the influences of the evil man has created, and there would be no sin for which to suffer consequences. This is the Truth.

"As I said before, Saint Ta, that is why your books are being written, to remind everyone that eternal life in God is within you, lying in wait to be acknowledged through the realization that all is one in the Christ Consciousness.

"Most humans, however, still have not learned to forgive themselves and each other. So they reincarnate over and over until, finally, they are able, through forgiveness, non-judgment and love, to release self-perceived karma and eliminate any possibility of new karma."

"Ah, Sweet Jesus, when You died upon the cross, did You, in any way, free us of our sins by removing our evil tendencies, our bad habits, ingrained in our natures through lifetimes of error?"

"Just by the condition of life on earth in the present moment, you can see that this did not happen. Many people still have bad habits and continue to sin through their free will even after being shown how to live in love. These sins keep them from God consciousness."

"Sweet Jesus, You say You came to forgive our sins and yet You say we should forgive ourselves. This is confusing to me."

"My life and death—this sacrifice—offers perfection for all time, a release of all karmic debt, forgiveness of sin known and unknown, for those who listen to the truth and live in love. For those who sin after receiving knowledge of this truth, there no longer remains a sacrifice for sins but a prospect of judgment, for so long as they continue to blind their eyes and cover their ears. I came to free the sins of all

through the message of truth and love. Some call it the good news. Even today, I have not abandoned you.

"My messages are simple to understand. To those who would hear, believe, and follow the message of truth, they will be increasingly inspired to release desires and live in love, in their daily living, toward all creation as one, with non-judgment and forgiveness of self and others, and to sin no more. The act of my dying on the cross and my resurrection, alive with the energy of the living God, along with the way in which I lived and taught, infuses people with this message of truth even today and inspires people to live in God. This way of life frees people from all karma, and they shall never perish but shall have everlasting life.

"My dying did not remove human tendencies toward evil or bad habits. But humans have free will to rise above the influence of bad habits. My way of living in love showed people how they could live beyond physical needs and desires. In my death is life, for mankind was and is given the chance to start fresh. Each day of your life, you are given the chance to start fresh. It is your choice.

"No man comes to the Father except through awareness of Christ Consciousness. This is the Way, the Truth, and the Life. This is the loving way of many—Christians, Muslims, Buddhists, Jews, Hindus and other religious sects alike— when they respect the equality of all people and beliefs. The Father is not limited to only those who believe in me, as Jesus the Christ."

"How can we be aware of Christ Consciousness?"

"By living always in love, you, naturally, grow more

aware of the presence of God in nature, self, Christed masters and all creation. In the presence of God lies your experience of Christ Consciousness. Live in unconditional love."

"Prior to Your coming, didn't people live in love?"

"In that time in history and pre-history, people lived in love with their own kind and did not always spread love to others less fortunate or of a different race, status, or religious tendency.

" I taught . . . love your neighbor as yourself. I taught . . . love your enemies as I have loved you."

"Sweet Jesus, it seems that some people need a personal connection to You or a living master for them to make these realizations."

"Ah . . . yes, Saint Ta. . . . For others it is as simple as experiencing love from God, which inspires them to go and sin no more and to live in love, as one with all creation."

"So we can go directly to God, instead of You or another master?"

"Yes. As I have often said before, some go direct to God. Some, instead, relate to a master who has passed over. Some are inspired by written word. Others need a living personal master, one they can attune themselves to, one they can verbally talk to and get encouragement from. Some accumulate for themselves teachers to suit their own liking. They often turn away from listening to truth and wander into myths. Everyone is at a different place on their path to final liberation in God. Remember, Gandhi said, 'In

reality, there are as many religions as individuals.' You are all uniquely different.

"What matters is that, whatever you do, do it with unconditional love."

"Even in Your physical death, You are alive to me as God is alive for me. You are as a companion in my life, and God lives in everything around and in me."

"There is no death. I am as alive for all people as God is for all of creation."

"If I enjoyed sin and evil, might I think that I could wait until the end of my life to seek forgiveness, knowing that, if I couldn't forgive myself, I still had chances with reincarnation?"

"It is exactly that way of thinking, along with mankind's idle actions, that caused the Church fathers to remove indications of reincarnations from the Bible. I can only say that the bliss of oneness and living in love with God is beyond the enjoyment of sin and evil."

"What do You make of the Catholic priests? I can't even put a name to it. I am at a loss for words."

"As I cleansed the temple, so I cleanse the Church once again. History does not paint a pretty picture of the Church. Its leaders and followers have engaged in wars, corrupted government, hidden abuses, fostered prejudice, and destroyed careers, far too long. The holy mission has often taken a back seat to arrogance, greed, cover-ups and power. The Church is reaping what it has sown. The Church's original teachings are still sound, and it is the

love and faith of good priests and, above all, the love and faith of the masses that keep the Church on its foundation. Without the faithful, the Church will crumble. This is an institution given to help mankind accomplish God's work on earth. It cannot teach what it does not practice.

"The conduct of priests and other laity in abuses, greed, egoistic arrogance and search of power has nothing to do with the original teachings of the Truth. It would be appropriate for priests to marry; however, the priests who are capable of sexual abuse, who are hiding behind the priesthood, may also hide behind marriage. Few are able to be celibate. The priests and the victims need treatment, and the priests will pay the price through karma, just as anyone else who has performed the same acts.

"To all perpetrators and victims of all crimes, I implore you:" Do not be afraid to cry out to God your doubts and fears and anger and questions and wants and needs. Let us hear you. Scream if you have to. Then ask, and you shall receive what you need. God has not abandoned you. God did not do this to you. Your situations were not unnoticed. Do not dwell on the memories. Remembering would only make it grow bigger in your life and in others' lives. Justice will prevail and love will conquer. Live in the present moment. Truly forgive self and others, so that you will not have to relive similar experiences again. Dwell in simple love toward all, especially yourself. Loosen those wavering thoughts and replace them with the love-filled light I give to you, from my heart to your heart. For I love you as my Father loves you."

"Do you believe that gay persons should marry and be able to be priests or ministers?"

"You must learn to see the good in everyone. Love unconditionally. No judgments, victimizing, and no comparisons. Gay persons are no better or worse than you or I. If they are not breaking God's laws to live only in pure love— mind you, I did not say man's laws—then there is no reason to intervene."

"Why are some people so prejudiced towards gays and others?"

"It is a comparative act. They are comparing that person as less than or different from their selves. Once they determine they are better, it is simply inflated ego. Even in your daily lives, when you talk of others, it is often in comparison to your own way of living and doing things. You are all equal in my Father's eyes—one no better than the other. Listen when I tell you, be aware and learn from your ego, as what you sow, you reap. As soon as you judge, you are comparing. Release the ego and dwell in love at all times."

"What are God's laws?"

"There is nothing about being gay in the laws of God, as were written in Exodus of the Old Testament and in the New Testament, which still hold true for today."

I stopped to look up the Ten Commandments in Exodus:

You shall have no other gods before me.

You shall not take God's name in vain.

Remember the Sabbath day, to keep it holy.
Honor your father and mother.
You shall not kill.
You shall not commit adultery.
You shall not steal.
You shall not bear false witness against your neighbor.
You shall not covet anything that is your neighbor's.

"Nothing in there about being gay or different than anyone else."

When George edited this chapter, he realized I only had nine commandments. Upon further investigation, we realized I had left out: "You shall not make yourself a graven image. . . ."

And so I asked, "Sweet Jesus, does this apply to pictures on the altar of You and other saintly personages?"

"Pictures, statues, icons serve as inspirations and reminders of what they represent, and are not for the purpose of worship."

Further, Jesus prompted me to add the following familiar commandments:

"You shall love your neighbor as thyself.
Above all else, you shall love God with all your heart, and with all your soul, and with all your mind."

Sweet Jesus, "How can we learn to live in love at all times? This is almost humanly impossible."

"The New Covenant speaks clearly of living in love. This would make needless all previous commandments. If

one were to live in love, there would be no disrespect, no killing, no adultery, no stealing, no lying, and no need for false Gods. Only love would prevail. I have said before that one must practice living in love. Yogananda will speak of reaching this state of love through the bliss of prayer and meditation. For now, practice loving more and more each day. For whosoever liveth in love will surely know God and will have everlasting life."

"Sweet Jesus, life on earth can be such a joy that I wonder if I really want to get off this wheel of life. Maybe I could just keep coming back to earth. Then, there are times when I feel a desperate need to get off this wheel of life and be with God."

"The wheel of life is just that. There is no death. There is only change. One reason why there are some who want so desperately to get off the wheel of life is that they feel so acutely the pain of separation from God or, like you, Saint Ta, they have remembered God and long for the bliss.

"I feel your deep longing for God, Saint Ta. God has drawn you to Him many times. It is your free will and desire to help mankind that stays you within the realm of materialism, lifetime after lifetime."

I could not go on. The thoughts that crowded my mind were of humanity that needs help. And yet the longing for God and the experience of God is so blissfully sweet that I want that too. I want that so intensely that it brings tears to my eyes. I know that humanity will go on and be aided by those still on their paths. Sometimes I think that situations or people can't get along without me, and yet I know better.

Life has taught me that lesson. Things simply do go on and survival happens.

I was suddenly feeling lonely. I went into the bedroom and sat on the edge of the bed with George, where he was meditating. I thought about leaving him to go to God. Could I part with him? Would I be with him in heaven?

I asked, "What about George? Is he ready?"

"Are you attached to George? You must live in the world but not of it. Detach yourself, and yet live in the world. Love George, but be willing to go to God when the time comes. I cannot tell you of George's future; only George knows. I can tell you this . . . your loved one is loved by God and I, and we are well pleased with him."

"Can we be together in heaven?"

"Possibly, and with many more."

"Why aren't You in heaven? Why are You here?"

"I am everywhere for everyone. There is no separation. Heaven is within. Heaven is not far away."

"Sweet Jesus, Oh Divine One, I treasure Your sacred presence. I treasure Your guidance. I love You. You have been my friend for all my life."

"Even longer."

I typed all that Jesus said, and in doing so, I realized that these were the most precious statements Jesus had ever said to me. He had said them in other words, but this time they hit me where they held my whole attention. How could I share these sacred words? This was private. I felt it deep within my heart. I held it there as if it were one of my children. While thinking on this, Jesus interrupted me. . . .

"Saint Ta, there is nothing you can take with you except love. You are love. You must leave behind knowledge for others to learn from, even the knowledge you hold dear to yourself. There will be some who will understand and some who will not. Write, with your creative freedom of speech, for the sake of all others, while you can."

"I love helping people and I also want to be with God. It's a difficult decision. Yet, recently, these experiences of longing to be with God are so strong I feel it deep within my heart, and it spills over into tears. Even in those moments I hold back."

"Saint Ta, fear is what keeps you from experiences of ever-higher grace. Do not be afraid.

"There is only love for someone like you who has the vision to see love, beauty and good in all things, no matter the situation, along with the courage to speak these truths. It is not to be my decision to lessen the path you have taken in this life or the path which you may choose to take in any future lives. Only you decide."

"I once looked closely into my bathroom mirror at my face. Nose to nose. I asked myself in the mirror, 'Who are you?' Again, adamantly, I asked, 'Who are you?' Face after face quickly flashed before me. The no-noise was deafening. One right after the other. Just like those instances on television where they flash view after view, faster and faster. I saw old people, young, every color and nationality.

I stayed with it as long as I dared. It was hard to tear myself away—physically and emotionally hard. The experience was so profound that I finally gasped at the totality of it. It was frightening. With difficulty, I physically had to push myself back, as if from a suction. What was this hold on me?"

"These people were your past lives, and in acknowledging them, they showed themselves to you, and you were drawn even further and further into the past. You have lived for eons. Enlightenment is ongoing for you. Your channels are fully opened. You have no bad karma. You can go to God any time you wish."

Jesus' words caused me to go within. I remembered His Holiness Cealo had also told me I have no bad karma. I found solace within, peace from my thoughts, worries and pain. A wave of energy enveloped me from the soles of my feet to my crown, flowing with a slow, pulsating warmth. Even as I write, it comes again, from my head, this time, and down to a suddenly-closed pelvic floor. Again and again it envelopes me. I am within and I am typing. There is no difference. I am here and I am there. My hands are tingling with energy as I type, as if they aren't mine. The energy flows with each breath. My breathing is as gentle as a sleeping baby's, even slower. In the stillness is oneness and joy. My body functions on, as I meditate in peace.

* * *

After a time, I asked, "Are You saying I could even go today?"

"Yes; it is your free will. However, must I remind you of

the work you are here to do."

"I remember times when I lost conscious memory of my body and everything around me, and yet, in a burdenless, unladen state, I had consciousness of a sea of glorious light. . . . I long for that always."

"We know."

"Do we ever reincarnate to other planets? What can we expect on other planets when we reincarnate? What kind of life forms are there? Are they similar to earth as far as dualities, intelligence and awareness is concerned? Is there suffering, war? Some people on earth seem to feel that we are so important that this is the only planet in the universe with life." The questions spilled out of me as if they were not of me. Still I was interested.

"Earth is not the only life-sustaining planet. Do not put limits on God.

"You must remember you are not your body; you are your soul. To survive in a different atmosphere, you would take on an appropriate form, fitting for all of your needs."

"How can our soul gain what it needs for self-realization on other planets?"

"There are vast universes out there, constantly changing, growing. Do not put limits on God or yourselves. To grow, one must accept the concept of change. You will be given new life form wherever you go, to provide you with experiences to gain self-realization."

"I have had experiences where I know I've had that

same experience before—same instances, same people, same surroundings—same thing as before. The first time I was aware of this was in high school. I remembered a dream or vision from early childhood of the same experience that was happening before my eyes. It was just an insignificant remembrance, nothing to do with anything. In my vision a teacher was sitting on a bar-type stool, showing the class a simple box. The teacher's desk had a sink in it. As a child, in this dream or vision, I remember thinking it was silly for a teacher to have a sink in his desk. I laughed at it. That is probably why I remembered having seen it before, as it was unfolding before my eyes later on in high school. The box was an antique camera.

"So I guess I am wondering, 'Why would this happen?' It happens a lot. As I grow older, I have more and more instances of this. They don't seem significant at all. It's almost as if we are living parallel lives, each in a different time-frame—as if I am living my life now, in the past and in the future. What is going on here? Is this deja vu?"

"Saint Ta, deja vu happens. Don't worry about it. It is not important. That is why, most often, only seemingly insignificant, unimportant events are remembered during deja vu.

"All experiences there ever were, or ever will be, are within your body, mind and soul. When you pull a past, present, or future experience out in remembering, it is like you are living it for the first time, yet all possible experiences are already there, in the present moment."

"How does this give us free will, if the future is already

laid out for us?"

"All choices that you could ever make are already within you. As you live your life, you make choices using your free will. In the moment of your childhood you were also in the moment of your youth. In present time there is no past and no future. And the past, for mankind, only remains as a memory.

"There is no fixed reality except for the light of God. Everything is all one, including time. This oneness dwells as the light of God, the only reality. In this oneness and light you dwell—with free will, by the grace of God—to increase the light of your soul through loving actions and to vanquish your darkness.

"Time for you and time for me may appear different. I am in the now, and you live mostly in perceived time restraints within the earth plane. Yet it is not unusual for you to experience the irrelevancy of time outside of physical consciousness. During meditations, you've experienced time as eons going by, when, in fact, it was only seconds in your time-frame. Other times, meditation seemed like seconds, yet was a longer period of time in your time-frame. You were experiencing the past and the future in the now, in oneness with all there is."

"I am noticing that, more and more. How can it be that I remember I was with Sri Yukteswar in my last lifetime."

"The book you will write with Sri Yukteswar is the reason why you opened up to that remembrance. Your consciousness is expanding."

"I don't know enough about Sri Yukteswar to write a whole book."

"It will reveal itself. All is within. You only need help in remembering."

Hmm. . . . That set me to ponder what is to come.

"I used to regress people to past lifetimes. It was sort of like a parlor game and it was fun until, one day, I regressed a person to a past-life tragedy that was traumatic. It was difficult to bring her back to the present time as a whole person. I was able to do it with a lot of help from Spirit. I never, intentionally, did regressions again."

"That was a good lesson for you. You made a wise choice. Living in the past and future does little for the present. Do not pursue seeking past or future lives. It is nature's kindness that you don't remember. It will come naturally, if at all. It must be handled with great caution, so that past and future weaknesses do not resurface or influence your present life. All that comes to you in this lifetime are things you have chosen to address now. Just live in the now. Just relax and smile. It has been said that a wise man forgets many things. Come on now, smile!"

"O.K.". . . So I smiled, then went on to say, "Some say that regressing can help a person in this lifetime, if something that might have happened in a past lifetime is being addressed now."

"Listen when I say . . . Forgive all the past, forget all the past and let it go, even the unremembered past. Go on, in the present, and sin no more."

"Jesus, I recently said to George, 'The past and the hereafter are not my favorite subjects for discussion, because they are not easy for me to talk about. They are too deep for me. Why would I want to be talking to Jesus about all this? I would not have picked these subjects.' And George said, as You have said many times before, 'This information isn't just for you. Other people will want to know.' Yet, I am uncomfortable with the subject matter at times. What You have revealed to me is profound, and yet, it still raises so many questions."

"Ah, Brave Heart, what we are addressing is important. It must be said."

So, taking a deep breath and going on as if drawn on, somewhat reluctantly, I said, "If I let myself think about choices of experiences, I am reminded that I wanted to be right there when the Berlin Wall came down."

"You were."

Surprised and interested, I went on, "Hmmm. . . . Is that why I was so overcome with emotion when I saw it on the news and later when someone gave me a piece of the wall? It brought me to tears. I wanted to cry, but I had company and they would not have understood. I keep that piece of wall in my night stand. How could I have been there?"

"All things are possible."

"Woah. . . . So, I have all of these choices I could consciously make. So, is that programmed in there? Are my choices really not free will? God gave me free will, but how come—like what has happened here with the déjà vu—how come I didn't have free will with that?"

"You did. Unlimited experiences, knowledge, circumstances and consequences are available to you and all others, as choices you make in this lifetime using your free will. How you have chosen to live those choices is entirely up to you."

"And what of the others? Do they make choices to fit into my choices?"

"It is all a part of the play of oneness. All your choices fit into all choices of others as if in a dance of life. Moment by moment, instantly, in the now, each of you are making choices to fit encounters and events whether alone or with others."

"So, how could I be in my childhood and in my youth at the same time?"

"All is now."

"What if I wanted an experience of going to Africa? I had always wanted to be a missionary in Africa. But not anymore. Missionaries seem to want to change the culture and religious beliefs of people. I believe even You said that if they have God, who creates and loves, that's all that is necessary."

"You are right. Still missionaries are needed for educating and, in many ways, improving the lives of others."

"If I wanted to have such an experience, is it in there? Is it in my computer bank?"

"Unlimited experiences are within you now—past, present, future."

"But we are stuck within a life we have chosen for now."

"This life you are living is the one you chose and are aware of for now. Still, often within your lifetime, changes were made."

"Do all humans have the same memory bank to draw from?"

"Yes. God created all in His image and gave you free will. God is unlimited; however, you are not consciously able to access all knowledge with your self-limiting abilities."

"So, then, why does a person in Germany have different experiences and language than I do, if we all have the same memory bank?"

"With your free will, you prearrange the choices of parental heritage and environment you want for your lifetime, based on your desire to fulfill karmic debt or to come back to help out certain situations. Just being born into a certain location will activate memory to assist you with that particular lifetime."

"I have always felt I was born to parents who gave me away to parents of my choosing who couldn't bear children. I am grateful for my birth parents for providing that opportunity.

"Do we ever leave things undone?"

"As long as you have desires, things will be undone and you will not be able to go to God. Once your soul is satisfied—non-attached . . . egoless—you do not have to rein-

carnate. You do not have to experience all things."

"I feel drawn to China. I can almost see myself there."

"Some of your energy from a past life remains there, seemingly drawing you."

"I was in China!"

"Yes, you were. Many times."

"Was I me? Was I Chinese?"

"You were Chinese and you were you—new incarnations of your one soul."

"So, do You think I fulfilled the China experience?"

"I tell you again, do not pursue seeking past or future lives. It will come naturally, if at all. It must be handled with great caution, so that past and future weaknesses do not resurface or influence your present life. Live only in the present moment."

"Have I been to Africa in a past life? Don't answer that. I really don't want to have these desires. It seems easy to get caught up in it. Sorry."

"No need to apologize."

And so, smilingly, I go within. My quiet breathing brought with it such an expanse of kundalini power that the muscles in my pelvic floor clamped shut, and energy burst upward into my head. The energy increased with each breath I took. I meditated. Time passed, as if nothing. I felt as if I had meditated long, and yet, it was a very short time. I love it when this happens.

Chapter Eight

Words

"Every one who is of the truth hears my voice."

—John 18:37

"Sweet Jesus, what is the Om sound?"

"Ah, Saint Ta, it is the creative vibration of God the Holy Spirit expanding the body of divinity, within you and all as one. It is the harmony of creation and destruction, between Mother Earth, Mother Nature, humanity, dualities, the sun, the planets, the universes and all of creation. It is the vibratory energy of the Holy Spirit preserving all that has been and is to come. The Om sound is made up of all vibrations, including the earth moving through space, the sound of one leaf falling and your silent thoughts."

Out of the depths of a deeply-sighed Om . . . I was speechless. . . . For a time I was still. Then I said, "Sweet Jesus, I wrote a poem about the Om some time ago. Would You like to hear it?"

"Yes, I would. I love poems."

"When You speak to me, it is beautiful poetry."

"I love to sing poetry, too."

Surprised I asked, "You sing?"

"Sure. So do you."

"Yes, a lot."

"Well, let's hear that poem."

Still intrigued, I continued, "Will You sing for me sometime?"

"I sing with you often."

"How come I don't hear You?"

"You do. Remember, you often marvel at the sound of someone singing disharmoniously with you, always a half a note under or above or both when you sing. When you connect with The Divine through your singing, you may hear within you, vibratory astral or causal sounds, nature spirits, creation, masters and more, singing with you."

Smiling I continued, "I love it when that happens. Why off-key?"

"To make you aware of spirit presence."

"When that happens, I always sense a presence with it. Often I sense Sebastian, a past-life master. At first I thought I was toning with my voice. Then I thought it must be spirit. I didn't know it might be You, too."

"If it were toning, others could hear it."

"Is the Om sound the deep resonating sound I hear?"

"Yes. Its collective vibratory sound is like a motor run-

ning smoothly, quietly and effortlessly. If you listen care-fully, you will hear and feel this Om sound from within your own self.

"This does not mean you will hear the word 'Om.' 'Om' is the closest word to explain the sound all creation makes, collectively, in one vibratory hum.

"Chanting 'Om' silently can help you focus on God and block out distractions while meditating. And then, in si-lence, listen and feel for the Om sounds within. This will open new doors to awareness of Spirit."

"Does one always hear the Om sound with their ears?"

". . . and with the heart and soul. For, within the changeless oneness, you may hear the tones of creation as a whole, with the heart and soul senses, not just the ears. Or you may hear the tones separately, given your state of consciousness or awareness."

"Is the disharmonious singing an Om sound?"

"The Holy Spirit's creational, vibrational 'Om' is made up of all sounds: physical, astral and causal. Individual sounds are not the Om, but are an important part of the whole. The state of consciousness you are in determines how you hear astral and causal sounds. Disharmonious singing, angels singing, deep sounds, high-pitched bells, knocking are just a few examples of physical, astral and causal sound vibrations that collectively make up the Om. Those in the astral and causal consciousness might only experience silence until they are able to hear with the heart and soul."

"When I hear the disharmonious singing, I find myself catching my breath quickly so I can continue singing, hoping it won't go away. The sounds bring me great joy and peace."

"Good, it should."

"That rhymes.

"Everything does."

"Are you saying there is poetry in everything?"

"If you listen carefully."

"That is truly beautiful, Sweet Jesus. I love sound and music. I have always said, the most beautiful sound in all the world is someone who can't hold a melody, singing for all they're worth. I love it."

"You do seem to like disharmonious music.

"Especially when You and spirits sing with me."

"Read your Om poem."

"That rhymes."

"Aren't I good."

"Mmmm."

"No, Ommm . . ."

SOUND OF THE GREAT OM

Almost inaudible,
The sound of Om . . .
From up the river came.
A monotone of breathless timbre,
Deep blend of octaves, still the same. . . .
OM . . .

Gaining strength and closer still,
The highest, lowest, and all between,
The Om sound rang within my heart
And spread to it a love unseen. . . .
OMM . . .

Severeness, blend of adoration . . .
A reverberating whisper fading . . .
To an expectant hush.
Up the river came the spreading
Om sound in its predestined rush. . . .
OMMMM . . .

It traveled fast and closer still. . . .
Gained in strength and voices too. . . .
The volume grew.
OOMMMMMM . . .

The birds grew quiet. . . .
Leaves stopped their sway. . . .
The wind was hushed
And held at bay. . . .
River ripples turned to glass,
And, as the Om sound passed,

The loudness threatening,
It turned ever so slight,
Acknowledging my beckoning
Upon the riverbank.
And I became, for one moment,
This minor monotone of tumultuous sound. . . .
And then it passed and traveled on.

The fading chant of OOMMmmmm
went on and on and on. . . .
And left in my soul eternal love. . . .
And the birds sang loud,
And the river rippled,
And the wind blew,
And the leaves swayed,
And the earth and my soul sang on . . .
Ommmmmmm . . .

"I sometimes wish I didn't have to catch my breath, and that the sounds that I make when I sing could last forever, or that breathing in the fragrances would last forever. It seems the breath constricts me. Sometimes, when I am meditating in silence or song, I have better breath control and can sing far longer between breaths."

"Yogananda will speak to you of breath control in your next book. Realize that all words are important—whether out loud or silent, of short duration or long—and they create and have an effect."

"That reminds me of an incident that happened to me recently. I was coming home from visiting with family. I timed my trip so that I would be able to buy my lunch at a market in Beulah that has vegetarian subs that I especially like. I bought the sub with the plan in mind to eat it in the car on my way home. When I got out to the car and opened the door, a fragrance that seemed of lilacs poured out and pervaded me. At the same time, the word 'death' came to me. In that one word, many were implied. I realized it was spirit telling me to be careful for the rest of my journey home.

"Needless to say, I was very careful, watching traffic and my own driving. After about an hour and a half of driving, I became very tired. Nodding off a bit, I shook myself awake. I realized I needed to pull over to sleep, so I watched for a likely spot where I could rest. I was finally drawn to a small cemetery. I pulled in, parked under some lovely trees, and feeling safe, I slept for an hour. I awoke refreshed and arrived home without incident."

"You are being cared for by many."

"I know. When I am aware of their presence, and even when I am unaware, I thank them. I love them all. And I love that You care for me, Sweet Jesus. Thank You.

* * *

"Are spoken words mightier than thought?"

"Words spoken are creative expressions from thought, and are strong because you are also sharing the words directly with another person. You are also creating thoughts in others through the spoken words, which are listened to, felt, and remembered. You are not keeping it only to your-

self. When you sing, Saint Ta, the sound and the words are infused with the One Creative Energy, needed to be heard by many to awaken their spiritual latency.

"Don't assume that written and spoken words are the only way to spiritual awareness. There was a time, long ago before words were spoken, when spiritual awareness came from silence. It was the only way.

"Even today, the experience of spiritual awareness is there for you to tap into through silence—in meditation, nature, and within yourself as you live your life in love. Opening yourself to your creative, listening self will help you be ever more aware of the divinity in words. Heaven and earth shall pass away, but my words will not pass away.

"Through the empowerment of written and spoken words, you continuously create. Even the sound of rain dropping on a roof has spiritual power, as nature is one with God and God is love."

I stopped to think a bit on what He said, and then I asked, "Jesus, if someone speaks of evil to me, are there thought forms that attach to me just by hearing the words?"

"If you let them. All words have empowerment. Consider what you are saying. Within the earth plane, where dualities are perceived, people don't realize that even their words are creative energy. When they are thinking or speaking loving thoughts, it creates love that spreads out into the world and back to self. But, if they are thinking or speaking negative thoughts, these, too, are spread out in your world and back to self. Imagine that you can reach out and grasp a thought. Think of it like that, that you have

created something that you could grasp and hold in your hand. It could be an evil thought. It could be a loving thought. It could be a happy thought. You have created something you have brought into your world by your thinking. These are the things you have to be careful about. The more negative thoughts you have about another person or even yourself . . . the more negativity there will be in the world and in your life.

"Think loving thoughts without judgment, and whatever you do, do it with love. Be the love that you are."

"It would be nice to be able to realize and remember everything that we read, see, hear, or experience. I might possibly be much-more wise."

"Wisdom is the fruit of experience from many lives. You are the sum total of all your lives. With each thought, word, and deed you are building who you are, and who you are going to become in the future.

"A wise person is one who uses experiences for good and not evil. It does not take a scholar to be wise. Knowledge, on the other hand, makes you responsible for the knowing. So one must be very careful with making conscious the knowledge from within. All the experiences there ever were, or ever will be, are within you. The more knowledge you consciously make known, through all learning experiences, the more you are responsible for knowing. If it comes in too fast or too much, it causes you great problems and difficulties in body, mind and spirit.

"Television is causing problems for your youth. Their minds are eager to learn, and yet they are not always ca-

pable of sorting out all the information. Often they watch violence in the real world as if they were watching it on television, unable or unwilling to react. Be very choosy about what you and your children watch on television. Monitor what is being watched and choose good programs, both fun and educational."

"Several years ago, I had occasion to witness a violent act, and I saw children, nearby, watching as if it were a movie, with no visible emotion. I was stunned more by that realization than the violent act itself."

"How people react to experience is as important or more so than the experience itself. Bringing violence into homes in the form of movies and sensationalized news broadcasts, and watching all of this from an easy chair, does not teach people how to react appropriately to their own experiences. They may even lose the ability to make sound judgments and decisions, because on television, all the thinking is done for them, and on television, you can turn it off or on. Some become excessively attached to the violence and its outcome, and nourish it by their thoughts, desires and words.

"By letting go and centering yourself into a oneness with all of God's creation, you can detach yourself from what is happening around the world and still be in it. While in this oneness, increase the light and love everywhere.

"Still, there are people destined to be a part of the action. Your light and love and prayers for these people are very important."

"When You speak to me, Jesus, I am usually able to repeat, over and over, the words You have spoken, so that I can record them. Other times, the thoughts are so fast they frustrate me when I am trying to type, and I cannot keep up with the input fast enough. Then I wonder if I am really writing what I am supposed to be writing. I thank You for your patience; however, I just wish my brain would tolerate faster verbal input/output."

"You are doing very well. What you write is what you are supposed to write. These words are of the Spirit and they will endure. If you abuse our words, we will let you know and you will not be able to write them. There are some who like to go on and on and abuse a topic, and like to hear themselves talk."

"I think that is true, yet I sometimes like to hear yogis compare their meditation experiences and share their knowledge. We learn from each other in this way, and it can be helpful. I especially admire the ones who are not boastful. I hope that writing of my experiences isn't being boastful."

"Ah, Brave Heart, your writings are being given a blessing. God is giving you courage and the ability to write with discernment, using words to share experiences and revelations, so that you might offer our words of hope. Since most of mankind is unable to hear in the silence, how is mankind to hear without someone to proclaim God's word over and over? Most people won't hear if no one talks or writes about it.

"Today, in your world, you and others are the voice of God. True spiritual words are scripture, even today, and

have the power of divinity and perfection. Your writings are filled with ongoing creative energy and will not be fruitless. These words are important and cannot be stopped."

"George told me that 'dabhar,' the ancient Hebrew word for 'word,' meant more than what 'word' means to us today. To speak was to express creative energy."

"That is true even for today. Out of the Creative Word, I became flesh and dwelt among you as a Son of God, an incarnate of Christ Consciousness. That is how powerful the Word is.

"In the beginning was the Word.
The Word was with God,
and the Word was God.
And the Word became flesh, mankind,
and the Word, as God, dwelt among us."

I had to stop and meditate on Jesus' words. Something didn't feel quite right. I didn't doubt what Jesus said; I just needed to find these familiar words in the Bible. I found them in the first chapter of St. John. The powerful message in the Bible was of Jesus as the Word which became flesh and dwelt among us. Here Jesus was saying mankind was made flesh from the Word, too, and the Word, as God, dwells among us.

It is hard for me when things like this come up. I treasure Jesus' words and I don't want to make light of scripture.

Before I got very far in my thinking, Jesus said, *"Ah,*

Saint Ta, there is no dishonor and there is nothing amiss here. You heard me correctly. The Creative Word is God. And mankind, too, became flesh, created by God from out of the Creative Word, and God does dwell as one with mankind and all of creation."

"Are we rewriting the Bible here?"

"Ah, no. The Bible, and especially the New Testament, has been tampered with far too many times. I only used this passage to show you how important the Creative Word is and that, further, the message is that all is one even as I am in you, and you are in me, and we are in the Father, the Son, and the Spirit, as one.

"Rest easy now, Saint Ta."

"It is different for me now when I read scripture in the Bible. I see so much more in it than I did before my awakening. It is as though I can read between the lines. I understand better the history of specific times in the Old Testament, which doesn't always relate to me in these times, yet I feel comfortable in that knowing. I best relate to the New Testament for myself and my times. It is ever more meaningful to me."

"Sometimes it seems pictures speak louder than words."

"Pictures create thoughts, which often lead to words."

"I never felt a need to have pictures of you, Jesus, because I have You so close within my heart. I learned the simplicity of being able to talk to You or God whenever I needed to. That's what comes from taking children to Sunday School or lessons or temple, to learn of God or masters

210 • Messages from Jesus

at a young age, so they can turn to God whenever they want or need to. I have held conversations with You all of my life. Once in a while, someone would come along with pictures or a rosary. But I never felt moved to have these objects. Some people would say they are a reminder to pray or talk to God. So my Catholic friends had rosaries, and I knew it was something they did, but I didn't really understand why they would need them.

"When I married George and we built a home here in the community, I knew he was going to want to have pictures of masters and saints in the house. Since I did not want these pictures in every room, we put a beautiful altar in each bedroom with pictures he wanted, including ones of You. My family pictures were limited to the hallway, my peanut gallery. And then, for whatever reason, competition or whatever You might call it, Sweet Jesus, I placed Your picture in just about every room in the house. It sort of reminds me of where I am in this sea of masters. I don't know about all of them. But now, I have Your picture in the dining room, in the healing room and, of course, in the bedrooms.

"I have this new habit now. I have been looking at the pictures in the evening, before retiring, to check for expressions on all the masters' faces. When I am not quite sure I did everything right in the day, I sense a loss of satisfaction on the faces in the frames. Since these masters are fully aware of my actions and thoughts throughout the day, their expressions tell me if they are pleased with me or not.

"When I look at Your picture, I never sense a feeling of dissatisfaction, nor do You ever make me feel that I could

have done better. It is always beautiful compassion. I feel
Your love for me, no matter what I do. It is such a pure
love, Sweet Jesus, that I am comforted, and then I pray to
do better. It's the kind of love that I know will always be
there. I can count on it. No hesitation. I feel that, no matter
what I do or what I say, You will be there for me. If no one
else loved me, You would."

"I am there for all people, for all time."

All grew quiet here. In the stillness, I suddenly realized
how powerful the words are that Jesus speaks to me. Before
starting this book, Jesus and I had never shared the problems of the world. Our companionship had been of a more
personal nature or as guidance in my healing work. And
suddenly, the implications of the teachings in this book, together with the knowledge that they are actually from Jesus, hit me like a ton of bricks. Further, the realization that
all of this is to be published frightened me.

Suddenly, a comforting blanket of bliss came over me,
wiping away the fears. Time passed. I asked Jesus to send
His beautiful rose fragrance to me if all was well. I never
before asked for the fragrance. It didn't happen. Instead,
with each intake of breath, I felt rush after rush of blissful
energy radiating throughout my body. In this bliss I felt renewed strength.

After what seemed like a long period of time, and yet in
reality was only a moment or two, Jesus said, *"Do not fear.
Only desire goodness and joy, for you attract into your lifetime what your desires are."*

I remembered a simple desire I had some time ago that was fulfilled immediately with prayerfulness. I was going to Western Michigan University and had taken a number of varied psychology classes, so I thought they would give me a minor in psychology upon graduation. People would say to me, "That won't happen," because it was a smattering of psychology classes. Even so, I thought it would be nice to have the minor. I called the psychology department for an appointment. I had plenty of spare time on the day of the appointment, so I decided to walk to the bookstore.

While I was in there, I bought a book on prayer. I started to read the book as I walked back across campus for my meeting. The book stated that, when you pray, ninety-nine percent of the prayer should be praise and thanksgiving, and only a tiny amount for asking. I really liked that idea, because I always find so much to praise God for. So I thought I would see how this works. As I walked, I prayerfully found a lot to praise God for in nature and even in my life.

I had just about finished my prayer, when I got to the office of the head of the psychology department. Just before entering his door, I asked, "Please, dear God, I would like to have a minor in psychology upon graduation." I walked in and approached this man's desk. I said, "These are the psychology classes I have had, and I'm about to graduate, and I would like to have a psychology minor. Do you think that would be possible?" He looked at the papers, shuffled them around, made some notes, and said, "That's it, granted." And out the door I went, with a big smile on my face.

This simple experience of prayer influenced me for life. Now, I always center my prayers on praise and thanksgiving. I don't ask for much; most times I don't ask for anything. I don't need anything. Even the birds in the forest are provided with love, food and warmth. Why should I doubt that God would provide for me?

Ever present, Jesus said, *"Pray simply in this way, in secret, adding your own words:*

Acknowledge God:	*Our Father who art in heaven,*
Praise God:	*Hallowed be Thy name.*
	Thy kingdom come.
Turn it over to God:	*Thy will be done,*
	on earth as it is in heaven.
Ask God:	*Give us this day our daily bread*
	And forgive us our debts,
	As we also have forgiven our debtors;
	And lead us not into temptation,
	But deliver us from evil.
	Grant us world peace.

"Remember to Acknowledge God, Praise God, Turn it over to God, and Ask. If you find yourself unable to concentrate on this structure, simply clear your mind, and Spirit will intercede for you with sighs too deep for words. For the Father knows of your needs before you ask.

"When you get past your doubts and open your will to God, you find that God provides an answer for all of your needs. You have to be alert and ready to hear and see the

help He sends. As you live prayerfully, and grow in oneness with all the universe, you will increasingly be able to manifest all you might ever want and need.

"Needs are highly overrated. Materialism is rampant in your world. Clear yourself of all of this excess baggage and your burdens will be lighter."

"This reminds me of something I read about answers to prayers:

Many of us lose confidence in prayer
because we do not recognize the answer.
We ask for strength, and God gives us difficulties
which make us strong.
We pray for wisdom, and God sends us problems,
the solution of which develops wisdom.
We plead for prosperity, and God gives us
brain and brawn with which to work.
We plead for courage, and God gives us
dangers to overcome.
We ask for favors, and God gives us opportunities.
This is the answer. —Author Unknown

"Many years ago, my late mother-in-law would say to me, 'How come I never see you kneel to pray?' I didn't feel the need back then, since I lived in Your presence. My companionship with You, Sweet Jesus, has been nothing but devotional. I couldn't explain that to her at that time. I really didn't totally understand it then. Yet I knew I lived in God's and Your presence all of the time. I believed it as if it were a natural thing.

"However, I am realizing ever greater and greater love

for you, Sweet Jesus. And now that I can't kneel, because
of my arthritis, I long to kneel more and more."

Suddenly, a wave of bliss came over me . . . like the
spreading of love throughout my body. . . . It reverberated
within me . . . enveloping me. . . .

There are not enough words in our language to give you
my experiences or to fully describe everything that happens
in these blissful moments.

*"There are no words to describe bliss. Still, others can
learn from you some of what is possible for them. Whether
in this lifetime or future lifetimes, others will have their
own blissful experiences when they are ready."*

I stopped. I had just stated that my love for Jesus was
"nothing but devotional," then I wondered if that were
really so. I live my life as if in the presence of God and Jesus, not separate, and I go about my daily living as if He
were at my side, without all the fanfare of adoration. I
asked Jesus if I was devotional enough. I turned my head
and looked out the windows and up at the vivid blue sky. I
gazed deep into the blue, and tiny pin dots of brilliant lights
were dancing everywhere. As long as I kept my concentra-
tion on the lights, they remained. If I started to laugh from
the bubbling joy, they disappeared. Tears rolled down my
face. I tried to stay as still as possible and gazed long at the
depth of the blue. In this gift and bliss was my answer.

* * *

"When His Holiness Cealo and his interpreter, Amica,
came to stay in our home, he told a group of us of a vision

he had of the landscape around our home here in the forest. He emphatically said, "Tomorrow, six strong men!" With those creative words and few directions to all of us, the next day came and seven strong men, some women and children showed up. He sent some of them out to make purchases, then organized the crew to plant forty-four lavender plants, widen a one hundred foot path, transplant some plants and a tree and build a portal at the beginning of the path. The portal is made up of braided alder branches arching over the path, supported by ten cedar posts on each side of it. He further envisioned this archway covered with flowering vines and, eventually, more and more hardy lavender, interspersed with cosmos, planted everywhere.

"Sweet Jesus, my mind holds so many beautiful memories of past experiences, and even thoughts of memories to come. My cup runneth over."

"Your mind has no limitations. It holds within, all possible experiences that are necessary for your physical, emotional and spiritual growth. In addition, your mind has access to all experiences and knowledge that the universal mind holds, for infinity, for all humans as a whole."

"A teacher I had while in college told our class that we have all the answers within. She passed out little pompoms that had eyes glued on them. She told us to set one on our desk during the test she was about to give, and when we couldn't answer a question, to look at the pompom and the answer would come, and it did.

"Don't we learn new things?"

"You think you learn new things consciously, but superconsciously you know everything. Everyone does. And, if you are one with everything, you will know that all experiences are there just for the having. Then you are living the knowledge."

Chapter Nine

Oneness

Duality is overcome even in this world
By those who fix their faith on Unity.
The perfect Spirit dwells in Unity,
And they in the Spirit.

—Bhagavad Gita (5:19)

Fall has descended upon us far too soon. The summer ferns and flowers have faded and fallen to the ground, making a brown carpet. Mother Nature gifts us with complementary autumn reds, oranges and golds, in the flowers and leaves on the trees. Every season, Mother Nature provides colors, perfectly coordinated, that are pleasing and uplifting to all.

We have invited the Retreat staff for a get-together here at our home this evening. They work hard at the Retreat and we like to prepare a meal for them once in a while. It is amazing to me to see these beautiful, young people so focused on their spiritual path. I often wish that I had had the opportunity to live in a retreat when I was young.

Ever present, Jesus said, *"Ah, sweet Saint Ta. These young people need that exposure to God, concentrated, in their now. Times are crucial and young, spirit-minded youth are needed. You did not need to be in a retreat to be surrounded by the remembrance of the One. You already lived the opportunity as you lived your life."*

"Why is it that I am at this Retreat now? Why in the autumn of my life?"

More to myself than to Jesus, I drifted off with my thoughts. . . . Someone had told me of Song of the Morning just after I had my awakening. I remember feeling a need to go there, and finally, in the third month of my recovery, I took the trip. My endurance was still poor, and the drive was more tiring than I had anticipated. Even at the Retreat, I often sat in the snow and rested in the silence from time to time, while trying to get from one building to the next. Thinking about resting in the snow brings back sweet memories and reminds me of a prose poem I wrote about my visit.

SONG OF THE MORNING

In the north country highland forests
of Michigan, on the Pigeon River,
at Song of the Morning retreat,
the elk run wild,
deer are abundant,
water runs clear, and
woodpeckers drum a beat.
Here the fairies and wee folk
must truly live.

I sat in the midst of the snow,
soft, deep, and glistening.
The sky, uncertain—
snow clouds to bright blue.

The days and I moved slow,
as if time stood still.
Body rhythms, leisurely delayed;
time . . . irrelevant;
only a breath from God.
My emotions,
overwhelmed by the beauty,
answered to frequent, soothing releases.

As I sat, I danced as if I were of the
northern lights, not human,
colorful and flowing in syncopation
with Mother Earth and Father Sky.

I was warmed by a glow in my heart,
embraced with healing love,
and sung to by people of God.

I slept the dark away and woke to light.
I was greeted by others of like mind.
The chanting and meditations were healing:
Praising God, Thanking God, Loving God,
Being one with all,
Losing myself,
Renewing myself,
Finding myself.

In the Retreat everyone is focused on healing, spiritual growth, God, masters, healthy diet and so much more, from a holistic (spirit-mind-body) point of view. The silence, the people, the energy are profound. Everything I ever wanted in my life is concentrated right here. God is nearly always on my mind in this atmosphere of spirituality and natural beauty.

"In this environment you have truly found your purpose. Your writings will not be in vain. Your experiences and awareness will teach others how to grow in love and one-ness with God."

Seemingly eager to impress Jesus, I said, "Sweet Jesus, I want to discuss the chakra system, which I have studied."

Without waiting for a reply from Jesus, I rushed on. "I realize that there are seven, possibly eight or more, major chakras (energy centers). I also believe that there are chakras at the tips of the fingers, toes, nose and in every joint of the body. For now I want to talk of the seven major chakras and the physical, emotional and spiritual levels. As an energy worker, I can feel irregularities within the chakras. I tell my ego to step aside, to stay it from interfering while I work with a client, until I am done. Once the ego is out of the way, it is easier to connect with what I am feeling. I prayerfully meditate while clearing their aura and, by the grace of God, issues are brought to the surface and often dissolved. Then the chakras open, and healing occurs.

"There seems to be a progression, for physical, emotional and spiritual growth, from the base all the way up to the crown chakra, each energy center building on the one before and yet related to all of them as a whole. Each chakra functions within many levels, from the physical body to the astral and causal bodies.

"One needs to lovingly forgive self and others daily in addressing dysfunctions related to a chakra. Then let go and let God."

"Love is at the root of all being. Nothing can be accomplished without love. When you forgive yourself, love replaces the wrong. When you live in the present moment, there is no past. Accept who you are in the present moment only. You are a child of God. God loves you."

"By placing my hands just off the first chakra at the base of the spine, I can help a client deal with issues of survival or sexual dysfunction that surface in the form of emotional releases from the client."

"Why do you concern yourself with survival? Even the birds in the air and the flowers of the field are taken care of by God. They do not worry about survival."

"When I place my hands on the second chakra, just below the navel, issues of dysfunctional relationships with others and self often come up. Clients seem to remember mostly the negativity, and they find it hard to forgive themselves."

"You remember the negative more predominantly because negative karma has already been created in you and subconsciously you know this. Do not hold onto this. Let it go. Forgive yourself and others and replace the negative with the good. If you have to, write of the good things you

have done and place them on your bathroom mirror, where so many of you seem to start your morning observing your natural face in a mirror. Then, going away, you at once forget what you are like. Look into that mirror—really look into that mirror—and forgive yourselves and love yourselves.

"If you continue to hold onto this negativity and fear, you will leave this world with it, and you will need to address it again. I tell you, replace it with love. And, I tell you, sink into the infinite oneness and do not dwell on negativity and unforgiving."

"When I place my hands on the third chakra, just below the ribcage, issues surface relating to self-respect, self-esteem, self-confidence and physical energy. Often things that bother people in relation to this chakra are things they did wrong toward self and others."

"All is right, in God's eyes!"

Still ignoring Jesus words, I continued on, "I often find good there too. An enhancement of intuition often takes place."

Suddenly, Jesus' words reverberated off the inside of my head, *"Listen to me. You are not listening. . . . Just stop and listen. . . . If you let go of negativity and practice living in the presence of God with unconditional love toward all, in each and every present moment, there will be no need to open the chakras. They will be open all the time. . . ."*

I stopped my rambling. A sense of relief came over me, as if a great weight had been lifted. I turned and looked out the window. I held my breath. In this present moment, all was still and golden, as the sun rose and radiated its gold-filled, fiery light onto everything. . . . It was as if nature had stopped breathing. Nothing moved. No wind whistled through the trees. The beautiful, golden stillness entered me and triggered joy, and in that joy, I sighed and I laughed! What a great joke we play upon ourselves! Laughter ruled.

Time passed. There was no need to comment on the other chakras. All that is ever required is love. I needed time to think about all that had taken place. "Don't hide your light under a bushel basket," Jesus whispered. He knew I was starting to wonder about all of this again. I was trying to justify all that I write. Not that it isn't truth, but to justify my sharing so much with you. And sometimes my enthusiasm gets out of hand and I don't know if it is really enthusiasm or ego. Still, I feel some things are too sacred to share.

Again He said, *"Don't hide your light under a bushel basket. It is your worry over what others will think that keeps these thoughts coming back to you. Do not bother with those egotistic thoughts. Ignore them. The ego serves you only to make you aware of your faults. Your fault is your worry. Set it aside. What others think will not change things. They will not cause you to lose what is most important.*

"Recognize that, when you are aware of the ego surfacing, it is showing you a situation you need to pay attention to and correct. How else are you going to be aware of problems you need to be working on? Stop worrying."

Humbled I said, "Thank you, Sweet Jesus. I understand what you are saying and I . . . will stop worrying. Funny, I really wanted to write, 'I will try to stop worrying.' I stopped myself in mid-sentence and changed it into an affirmation. I'm feeling really good about being able to do that."

"Good! You are learning. Manifestation comes with sound intentions."

* * *

"Ah, Sweet Jesus, since coming to Song of the Morning, my closeness to God has grown and I've increasingly experienced the oneness. It's as if the experience of oneness grows with us as we progress spiritually."

"As you realize and feel your oneness with all things, you become more and more aware of living in the presence of God.

"There are many degrees of oneness, and people experience oneness differently. It is not easy for all people, young or old, to become aware of the oneness of all. I think it would be good if you would share your experiences. It may help others to start to feel this awareness."

"I can only explain how it is for me. I am not sure it is the same way for everyone. I would need you to guide me, so I don't go off on another tangent.

"I am always at your side, Saint Ta."

Smiling warmly within, I began. "My daughter used to do a form of art work called pointillism. The whole picture is done with dots. Starting with one dot, forms take place as she adds more and more dots. The art work may become a rose on a stem or a castle in the air. Yet, the whole of the picture is made up of dots, forming certain basic characteristics, each dot becoming a part of the whole. Imagine all of creation, including ourselves, as made up of dots. All of these dots, the size of sub-atomic particles, give us physical form and are also the substance of our far-reaching, nonphysical being, the aura. These particles/dots act like life force energy waves.

"Please correct me if I am wrong, but I believe all we are and all we have ever experienced is encoded within each particle."

"The essence of your aura, within your body and beyond, is your life force, which carries memory from your life experiences."

"These dots/particles/energy waves are constantly in motion, radiating near and far, into earth's atmosphere and even beyond, decreasing in density as they go farther and farther out from the body. You are as a seed, and your aura the branches, and God the blossom, still all one. We are connected with each other and all things by our mingling auric particles, or waves of energy. We mingle with our neighbors, loved ones and all of creation, without discrimination."

"You are one with God everywhere. You are remembered. Each particle, as a wave, carries all your ongoing memory, for sharing within group consciousness and for individual and divine communication. Remember the 'one hundredth monkey' principle?"

"Is that the story of monkeys on one island, surrounded by water, who suddenly decided to wash their food in the ocean to rid it of the sand? When enough of them were doing this, the monkeys on another island started doing the same, without any kind of instruction from the first group of monkeys, even though for centuries, they had not washed their food!"

"Yes. The group consciousness of the monkeys invoked the same response into the group consciousness of the other monkeys. To go even further, the consciousness of this universe invokes similar response for all creation and other universes reciprocally.

"One person cannot change the whole world of the collective experience at once. But one person can be a seed from which group consciousness will grow. Each of you could be that seed to generate a new world based on love and peace.

"Sweet Jesus, what is in the space between the particles of the aura?"

"Love, as waves of light and life force, permeates your whole being, including the physical body as well as the astral and causal bodies, filling the spaces between and within the particles and beyond into all creation. The more love you give to God, yourself, others, and all of creation the more intense the light and love is you receive in return, hence the healthier you are in mind, body and spirit.

"The love you have in your heart is the same love that is shared by all. The love that each of you carries within and out into the atmosphere is the same love you share with

your perceived lowliest of persons. There is nothing to separate you.

"God, as love and life force, is infinite oneness of all things, seen and unseen. God as love is already with you, in you, before you, beside you, and behind you, and you are in Him. You are that important to Him. He is all things to all people, no beginning and no end. It is already . . . all . . . ONE. Again I say, all beings in one are also within the Son of God, or Christ Consciousness. I am in you, and you are in me, and we are in the Father, the Son, and the Spirit, as one."

"You say love is also life force. When a person is dying and life force is withdrawing, does this mean love is withdrawn?"

"You are not abandoned. You are not wholly your body. The soul is continuously nourished from the light of your love, and you, as love, live on in full consciousness, growing ever closer to the final absorption into God. The magnitude of love given from you and to you during your lifetime determines the intensity of the love and light your soul receives.

"Love shines brighter within you when you are loving. If you are unloving, you do not lose love. It is only dimmer, awaiting the chance to shine brightly, once again, when you begin to grow in love."

"Speaking of brightness, Jesus, sometimes I experience phenomena with a vivid super-awareness. It seems unearthly. The sky is bluer, the greens are greener. Everything is so intense. The world seems lit up, not as though the sun were brighter, but as if each item were distinguished with sharper imagery and refinement. It leaves me breathless. I never know when this is going to happen. It can happen during a meal with others or when I am outside in the forest . . . anywhere. It seems to be happening more and more. Sometimes I see tiny sprinkles of light, like snowflakes falling through the air as if they come out of the depths of the sky, even in the summertime. What is happening?"

"It is there for everyone to see. Few are able. These happenings are blessings and an increased awareness to which you and others are opening."

"It makes me feel blissful and full of wonder! Sometimes I feel that way when I sing. I am so melded into the music nothing else exists. I could sing forever."

"Ah . . . Saint Ta. Your merging with the music is heavenly to hear. You magnetically draw others into the blissful, meditative oneness with you. Do not hide this under a bushel basket."

"When I sing ancient Sanskrit chants, not knowing the meaning of the words, I seem to concentrate more on the sound and vibration of each word. Feelings for the words seem to come from some unseen source. I like a translation, but without one, I feel freer to embellish the words with energy. I feel more blissful oneness in the vibrations of sounds."

"All people feel bliss, and in those moments, they feel oneness, often unrecognized. It is those high, profound moments that are unexplainable by the human vocabu-

lary—seeing a new-born baby, a beautiful sunset, a moun-tain for the first time, or hearing moving music—that give people momentary bliss."

Teasingly I asked, "So, in order to feel bliss, might I say to some people to continue looking for sunsets or having babies or listening to music?"

"Saint Ta, you know that is not the answer. Environ-mental stimuli do not last. Music can be shut off. The sun-sets come and go. Lasting bliss lies within and comes from experiencing and merging with the oneness of God."

"I wonder if this is why some people are addicted to drugs. Drugs may give them the memory of bliss, even though it is temporary?"

"Yes, but what the person doesn't realize is that the soul will never find contentment in abusive addictions. If they aren't able to turn their lives around, they must ask their selves if they really want to experience addictive lifetimes over and over. They must break this pattern now. Medita-tion is the easiest way to find bliss, and seeking outside help is an important first step."

"I often teach others how to clear their aura of negativ-ities and harmful entities, and I clear my aura daily. This helps me remove the negative energies and thought forms created by me, as well as those picked up from others, in-cluding those of addiction, attachment, ill health, destruc-tive emotions, or sadness."

"Explain how you cleanse your aura."

Hesitating only momentarily, I began, "There are several ways, but it is most important to start with a positive intention. Don't use terminology such as 'I wish' or 'I hope.' Simply affirm 'I' in a statement such as, 'I cleanse my aura of all impurities.' This makes a strong statement. 'I wish', 'I hope', or even 'I am willing' (to cleanse my aura) indicates that you are not doing it, just wishing, hoping, or are willing to do it. You need to set the intention with an active, positive affirmation.

"Or if you are able, just know and believe you are already cleansed in body, mind and soul and thank God for it."

"Remember, the will is strong. When you will something to happen and know without a doubt it will happen, it happens. Be careful how you use the word 'will.' There is a big difference between saying, 'I am willing' and 'I will.'"

"My mother used to say, 'Where there is a will, there is a way.'"

"That statement alone speaks volumes."

I knew how this could be, even though Jesus did not elaborate. I waited and nothing more came forth, so I continued to explain about cleansing the aura.

"Cleansing the aura in the shower takes the least physical effort. It is a simple act for the busy, tired, or ill person. Even though I feel fine, I sometimes begin or end my day doing this. I know the cleansing is underway as soon as I affirm:

I cleanse my body and aura of all
negativities and impurities,
rendering them harmless.

"Repeat your affirmation as many times as you are moved to do so. Saying it once may feel right. Just know that all negativities and impurities, including disturbing thought influences from yourself or others, are washed and drained away through your showering process. You might want to put up a written affirmation in the shower so you don't forget. I rarely do this while taking a bath. It feels as if I am washing the impurities into the bath water with me, and the thought makes me feel uncomfortable. Sometimes I simply shower off after a bath, using the above words with visualization.

"If you think loving thoughts, do kind deeds, and keep God uppermost in your mind, your aura will be clearer and you will feel healthier."

"Since your aura magnetically picks up on negative energies, consciously cleansing the aura, daily, is as important as cleansing your body. The intention in the act of cleansing the aura extends to your far-reaching aura, even when seemingly only done in your surrounding area. Your astral and causal connection with your extending aura allows this."

"After I was discharged from the hospital, following my awakening, I would light candles, put on soft music and, covering myself with a blanket warmed in the dryer, lie down on the healing table, wrapped in the wings of my pink angel. I did not have the strength to raise my arms to bring them down my body to clear my aura, so I simply set an intention and prayed to God to help me. Listening to the music, I imagined myself dancing with spirits as they cleansed my aura. I feel this is one reason why I recovered so quickly.

"Now that I am recovered, I usually cleanse my aura with movement. You may wish to use this method yourself.

"Put on some relaxing music. Settle yourself comfortably on the edge of a chair, or stand. Set an intention. Ask that all negativities be taken where they will not harm anyone or anything. Listen to the music. Feel the music and move with it, or simply imagine you are dancing amongst the northern lights or something similar. I call this 'dancing with the spirits.' While dancing, slowly clear the aura of negativity with your hands or mind. Start from the top of your head and slowly, rhythmically, work through the aura surrounding you, casting negativity downward and off your body. Let your intuition or hands guide you. You may feel irregularities, sense a wall that momentarily halts the movement, or feel something cold, hot, thick, tingling, or even an emptiness, just to name a few of the possible sensations. You may feel nothing. This does not mean that nothing is there. It just means you are not yet able to feel energy. Do it anyway. Relax and let your intuition and your hands guide you. When you come to an irregularity, whether felt or sensed, smooth it out. I sometimes do an erasing movement, and I also grab and toss. Keep smoothing it out. It is very relaxing and I love doing this. I feel so good when I am finished.

"If something doesn't seem to want to move out, command it to leave. If it still doesn't want to move out, ask if its presence remains for your highest good. If it persists and feels right, let it stay. If your intuition tells you differently, emphatically demand that it leave. It will leave.

"Several years ago, I was visiting my son; his girlfriend, who was very skeptical of my healing gift, was getting ready to go to work in a fast-paced bar. She came into the living room to talk to me, and told me she had to make eighty-three dollars in tips because she had to cover a check she made out for her car insurance. I said to her, 'Put that thought out there.' She also implied that the job was very stressful and she had a hard time when things would get hectic. I told her and demonstrated, 'When you become really stressed, excuse yourself and go to the bathroom, and, while there, say to yourself, 'I cleanse my aura of negativities and stress.' Place your hands above your head and, with your hands off your body, very slowly bring your hands down your head, down your body, and off your feet and arms, as if you are washing your body but not touching it with each stroke. Do this for as long as it feels right. This might be one time, or you might feel like you need to do it several times. You might feel a need to shake your hands off, or do erasing motions, or grab and toss.'

"The next morning, as I was sitting in the living room, she came in to talk to me again. She sat on the floor in front of me and poured out all of her tip money onto the carpet. Excitedly she told me that, when things got really stressful in the bar, instead of going into the bathroom, she put up her arms and shouted, 'Stop, everybody! Stop what you are doing. Clear your aura.' Everyone in the bar, while laughing, started following her direction! She said the whole atmosphere of the bar became pleasantly cheerful. By the time she finished telling me this remarkable story, she had finished counting her tips and had exactly the amount she needed to cover her check!"

"Ah the powers that be! Does anything surprise you any more?"

"Very little. Sometimes, when I want to feel blissful oneness with all, I mentally imagine and feel myself as all my energy particles, dispersing out as the aura, mingling with everything. I set my consciousness out there, not confined in my physical body. Sometimes, suddenly there is no body that I am aware of! I am not even aware of letting it go or willing it to go; this just happens.

"Sometimes, not only does my body disappear, but everything material is gone, and I am consciously aware of only indescribable bliss and joy. I cannot put into words how wonderful this is. I don't know why it ends, for I am simply brought back into body consciousness."

"You are in the world—self-realized, within the causal body and plane—but not of the world when this happens. You are living more fully in your expanding awareness because you are open to it. It is your state of being at this time. Remember I said, you do not lose the awareness you gained from one life to another life, however little or much it may be. This is why you experience my presence so acutely. It is the real world for you. What is felt by some as normal is body consciousness, with little awareness of living in oneness with God. You are intensely awakening to that which has always been, and exists together with the perceived world.

"This awareness is there for all people to experience

when their time is right. If people would lovingly let go of earthly attachments and forgive self and others they would be increasingly aware of oneness with God.

"People tend to back off just when they are about to experience this oneness, as if afraid or they feel unworthy. They might experience a wall, which seems insurmountable. Runners experience this when they run marathons. They hit a wall and have to push themselves to get through it. Once they do, they are able to continue running while experiencing a euphoria, similar to breaking through the wall into oneness and bliss. More and more people are awakening to this revelation. Do not be afraid."

"There is still conscious awareness when there is no body. I want it to last forever. I have not been able to remain in this state for a long period of time. And yet you say, I am ready to go to God. I have not been in a breathless state for a great length of time. I cannot elevate myself off the floor. I cannot do all of the techniques taught by yogis. I ca . . ."

Interrupting me, Jesus quickly said, *"What makes you think all of this is what brought you to experience God. Before your awakening you were not consciously aware of techniques, samadhi, or the yogic way. Still you experienced oneness with God. There are many paths to God. Your way is simply living your life in love, forgiving others and self, and believing that God, as the Father, Son, and Holy Spirit, is always with you. I say, God so loved the world that He gave His only begotten Son, as Christ Consciousness, that whosoever believes in him shall not perish but shall have everlasting life."*

This cleared my doubts. I was about to say something more to the readers when Jesus interrupted me again, *"Saint Ta, share that which may help others."*

I was moved to say, "When you feel oneness, stay with it and don't be afraid. Sometimes the experience of oneness just happens out of the blue. Other times I use visualization to experience oneness."

I settled myself and began. . . .

"Quiet yourself. . . . Close your eyes. . . .
Take a deep breath . . . sigh. . . .
Breathe slowly and center yourself. . . .
Go within. . . .

Slowly, gently, imagine you can feel yourself dissolving into a vast number of particles . . . beyond counting. . . .
Feel this aura of energy particles . . . inside yourself and outside yourself. . . .

Still, you are breathing . . . and with each outward breath you disperse . . . more . . . and more. . . .
With conscious thought . . . concentrate only on dispersing with each outward breath. . . .

Take your time. . . .
Breathe in. . . . Breathe out. . . . Disperse your particles ever outward . . . as you breathe out.

Feel how you shine . . . each little particle becoming a light . . . radiating outward into your surrounding area and even further. . . .

Feel the energy. . . .

Put your mind out in the aura. . . . Don't make it so hard.

Simply put your mind out in the aura. . . . You are not wholly your body. . . .

You are out of your body . . . as energy particles . . . separate . . . safe . . . with sense of self and conscious thought. . . . You are yourself . . . radiating love . . . as your own particles . . . everywhere. . . .

Imagine other objects and people dispersed. . . . Feel the blending of their auric energies with yours . . . reciprocally without discrimination . . . unified as a part of the One.

Radiate love. . . . Feel responses to your love coming back to you. . . . Increase the love. . . .
Feel this love return to you. . . .

Sense the rhythm. . . . As you breathe, so does all creation breathe. . . . Creation has a pulse . . . feel it within. . . .

You and I and everything are one with all . . . one with the world. . . . Blanket it with peace . . . love . . . and light all encompassing. . . .

Think of a person you know who needs healing . . . knowing their aura, too, is dispersed. . . .
Using your thoughts, magnetically attract that person's particles to you or yours to them. . . . See them before you.

Feel your oneness with them. . . . Distance does not matter, nor does time.

Merge with them . . . and feel and know where they need healing . . . or comfort. . . . Fill them with love and light . . . and healing thoughts.

Feel your own dispersed particles and fill yourself with love . . . and light . . . and healing thoughts.

Gently bring yourself back to present time."

* * *

"You may feel dark energy also. Still, everyone, every situation, and everything has light, some dimmer than others. Concentrate only on the light, even if you can't see it, and increase the light in all things with love."

"I often tell people, 'When you get too close to some people and feel as if you want to back off, you are feeling their auric particles as negative energy merging with your energy, and this may be uncomfortable. Or you may pick up positive, loving energy and want to hug them. Sometimes, after visiting a mall or theater or even the grocery store, I feel a need to brush myself off, and as soon as I can get to a more private area, I do so. It really works. If you can't feel the energy, do it anyway.' Many people tell me how well it works for them. Soon they are able to recognize discomfort as a sign that they need to cleanse their aura.

"Negative energies may manifest in our physical, astral and causal bodies as physical, emotional, or spiritual problems. Positive energies make us feel happier and healthier. And the kind of company we keep has a lot to do with the kind of energies we are exposed to."

"When you think a negative thought, your aura attracts other negative thoughts, which in turn, creates greater negativity. When thinking about any situation, those thoughts escalate as others join in that same way of thinking. The more people you have thinking about a situation happening, the greater the chance that it will. Group consciousness of a nation invokes similar response in other nations. Television feeds into group consciousness and makes it more powerful. Globally, divine intervention and human intention in love and prayer, slows down or halts negative action. As this love grows, its light shines ever-brighter and affects all things."

"People often ask if I protect myself. Most of the time I just know that I am protected. Other times I feel a strong need to do more. I call upon my pink angel, and she wraps me in her wings. Or I imagine being held by You, Sweet Jesus. Sometimes I simply pray to God for added protection."

"See, Saint Ta, you are a good teacher."

"I feel your guidance. Thank you, Sweet Jesus.

"Does everyone have to have an awakening to go to God?"

"Not at all. Your awakening was a gift to you, to ready you for the work you came to do. You were ready to go to God before this lifetime but chose to come back to perform specific work."

"Oh Sweet Jesus, I wish all people would have these experiences."

"Your writings will help."

"Why would I choose this task? I am a mere grand-mother."

"You started on your path with much less remembered awareness than you have now, and you grew. Saint Ta, for you to share is a gift. Your sharing teaches, and gives encouragement and hope to all who listen. As I said before, it is especially important now to reach those whom the messages will inspire and give comfort. My words and the words of the Father abide in you.

"To all I say, spiritual growth happens when you are ready to open yourself to the oneness of God and all that is, and live a life of love. All people are equal, one no better than the other. No matter where you are in life, you are where you are supposed to be on your spiritual journey. The presence of God is there for all people. It is the way you experience the journey that is important."

In my hesitancy to share, I had stopped short. I wanted to teach, but I didn't want people to think I feel I am better than others because of my experiences. In trying to sort this out, I felt a humbling feeling spreading through me. It subdued me for a few minutes. Then came a renewed urgency to continue.

"I once had a beautiful set of four small books, Spiritual Unfoldment, by 'White Eagle.' I thought I had bought them because they might look good on a small shelf I had. One evening I was going to settle in to read, and I picked up the first book in the series. It made no sense to me and I could not get into it. I was not ready to grasp what was written.

Some time later, I was packing to go out west for three months to work, and for some reason I packed the books, probably thinking, because they were small, they wouldn't take up much room. Once I got to New Mexico and settled in, I again picked up the first book. It was simply amazing. I understood everything in the book and then raced through the others. I was finally ready for what was written.

"This is how it will be with people that read your books. They may not be completely understood in the same way by all the people. They may not be ready for all of this. They may not be able to believe. Others may need to read it over and over. Still others will understand because they are ready. Your books are a treasure of what is old and what is new."

"Why do you say, 'are a treasure'? I haven't written them yet."

"The beginning and the end are in the present moment."

"I wish it were that easy, and I could remember it."

"You can."

"How?"

"By stopping for a moment. . . . Just be in the present moment. . . . Listen to all that is around you. . . . Meld into it. Don't try so hard. Relax. . . . Just breathe deeply the fragrance of nature as it is. . . . Feel the heat given off by the wood stove. . . . Listen to . . ."

". . . George stirring his cereal. . . . Birds are singing. . . . The refrigerator motor is running softly. . . . The tinnitus in my ears continues. . . . My breathing is loud. . . . The wind is howling outside. . . . I know the books will happen. . . . I see them. . . . I see myself as author. . . . It is in the NOW!!"

I seemed to be coming back from a long way away. That present moment was immense in all that it held. I felt like I had visited the inbetweens of that present moment. I had taken over the visualization from Jesus and was left with just me. I saw the books, done in completion. I did not open them. That is still to come. I am breathing easier now.

"Practice seeking present moments every chance you get. Simply stop, center yourself and go within, quiet yourself, and listen to your breathing. Direct your consciousness inward. Be aware. God-centered, simple yet marvelous, revelations will be made known to you."

"Jesus, I love how you make these things known to me, and yet, I do not want to look into the past nor do I want to see into the future. I would just like to be me for now, here and now."

"It takes no effort to be in the present moment. While in the present moment you are given revelations, effortlessly, which radiates into your consciousness.

"It is the veiled human condition that binds you to earth's time and space. As you grow increasingly spiritual, you will be able to release the limitations this boundedness has on you, and you will free yourself into the consciousness of oneness, timelessness, and unlimited revelations and still be able to function on the earth plane."

"Is this for everyone? What about the handicapped and ill persons? Will they be able to experience all of this?"

"Let me repeat . . . there is a special place in the heart of God for the infirmed. Again I say, God so loved the world that He gave His only begotten Son, that whosoever believeth in Him shall not perish but shall have everlasting life. It is as simple as that. The infirmed will experience letting go and letting God take care of them far sooner than the young and fit. They, too, live in the presence of and in the hands of God."

"I have read Your beautiful words about belief many times. Each time they give me great comfort. Yet, some wonder if we don't already have everlasting life after life in reincarnation. Is it really so simple, that if we believe in the Christ Consciousness, we will not perish? What does perish mean?"

"Some of you assume the lifetimes after lifetimes that are played out on the earth plane is the life everlasting that is spoken of here. Again and again I say, all beings in one are within the Son of God, or Christ Consciousness. I am in you, and you are in me, and we are in God the Father, the Son, and the Spirit, as one. In the realization of this consciousness of one, lies life everlasting, oneness with God and in God."

"Some question what belief means? Is simply believing enough? Is there more?"

"You will not get very far just sitting it out, thinking you have it made just because you are a believer, while doing

nothing to support it. Believing is more than thought. Believing is love in action. Love of self and others. Forgiveness of self and others. Living while feeling and being in the presence of God. Your belief, as a process of awakening ever more to the love and mysteries of God, will make you whole. Never losing sight of God is true belief."

"I remember when a pastor in an adult Sunday school class wanted us to relate how, sometime in our life, we lost sight of God. That we were angry or whatever and lost faith. And they were going around the circle, telling about horrible things that happened to them which caused them to lose sight of God. Then he came to me, and I said, 'I've never lost sight of God'. He said, 'Surely you must have lost sight of God'. 'No, I have never lost sight of God'. 'Come on now, yes you have. You must be in denial. With all that I know you have gone through, you must have lost sight of God somewhere. Everyone does.' I easily repeated, 'I have never lost sight of God.'"

"This is one of your strengths."

"Oh . . . I have not lost sight of God, but I am not perfect. I realize my perfection in the eyes of God, but within that perfection lies what I perceive as imperfections."

"Who said you had to be perfect? It is above the human person to realize their perfection because of their lack of being able to forgive themselves and others. Let it go. Realize and know that you and all others are perfect even in your imperfections, in the eyes of God. Relax now. You are a child of God."

Time passed. I stopped for a while, meditating on what Jesus said. Slowly I felt myself release the hold my moral upbringing had on me. Feeling freer and more relaxed, I could see what it was that was holding me back from realizing that my perfection in God's eyes is the same perfection I needed to feel within myself. As all my perceived imperfections loomed before me, I simply canceled them from my mind. Some came forth over and over, and each time I erased, zapped, canceled them. Soon they were gone. I was left with a feeling of peace and a wave of love enveloped me. I laughed.

Looking out the windows I felt joy watching an unusually-early snowfall. The dancing snow led me to write . . .

NATURE'S WINTRY WHISPERS

Nature has a wintry song.
Its whispers come in little winds
that blow the snow from trees
and make a glittery, misty fall
in all the shimmering breeze.

The whispers whistle a tune for me
as, lightly, snow swirls round,
and comes upon my lashes still,
and the top of me on down.

Its showy sounds show much more strength,
and whirling snow dances all around.
It's all blown up and back and forth,
and sometimes even down.

> Windless now, no tune sings,
> yet memories still hum my ear,
> as, soundlessly, the music rings
> within the silence I hold dear.

"Well, Sweet Jesus, that poem just came up . . . one, two, three."

"Good one!"

Here in this forested retreat, we live in retirement. It is several hours before daybreak. The stars and the moon are shining down on the snow, and in turn, the glittery snow is shining back. I am aware of unseen nocturnal animals moving about, even before I see tracks in the moonlit snow. The wind is still, and the birds are sleeping. I love these quiet, still times here in the forest.

George stays up late. He is a night person. I retire early. This way we both get alone time. Even with this schedule, there are still many opportunities for companionship. We love this arrangement and each other. George and I are so attuned to each other that some moments are anticipated before they happen. Often, we pick up each other's thoughts. We rarely tire of each other or of the ever-changing scenes before us. George takes good care of me in all ways, unceasingly.

When I go to bed at night, I can't wait to get up in the morning. Morning is my favorite time of day. When I wake up, there is an awareness of God already present, thus I don't always feel the need for disciplined meditation, for the realization accompanies me everywhere. It's as if I were two people, one attending to daily activity and the other ceaselessly aware of God. Right now, I feel like writing. God gave me the opportunity, at this stage of my life, to be in this quiet retreat to write. I use the time in wonderment. Often the words come quickly and easily, as if they are given to me.

Before retirement, I was given time off when I prayed for it. An awakening, which the doctors diagnosed as a stroke, not realizing the cause, kept me from working for four months. During that time off, I wrote the following to friends:

Dear Ones,

Today is Sunday. I will be home all day. Can't go anywhere. The day I came home from the hospital, the local theater director came over, not aware that I had just been released from the hospital. He offered me the alto solo in St. John's Passion for Easter at the Ramsdell Theater. Then he watched me walk like a drunken sailor. So I mourn another loss. I can't sing and I can't coordinate two hands at the piano, and have been playing one hand at a time, so I don't lose more skill. Even that is hard and slow, and the music does not feel very familiar.

I feel a major paradigm shift and intuitively believe it is connected to my recent physical impairments and . . . I will be led to a higher creative consciousness by flowing with it. My confusion helps to soften the total effect. I trust all will be okay, no matter what happens.

I had a wonderful meditation again last night. The spirits were with me. I asked them to enfold me to protect me from other spirits wanting a weaker, lighter spirit. I asked them to stop up energy leaks and to rid me of entities. I feel too weakened and vulnerable to do this myself. They are so still and they don't give me many answers. I feel intuitively that I am made to rest. For nearly four years now I have worked to enlighten others to God's healing grace. I am not telling you this as an egotist. I am only trying to explain my intuitive thoughts presently.

God is not giving me answers to the question, "What next, Lord?" because if He told me, I would become busy with preparation and He is forcing me to rest. Gently, subtly, but making sure I rest. My intent, when asking God for some time off, was to meditate to determine what next.

It seems I am going to be leading that sedentary, isolated, meditative life much sooner than expected. If, in doing so, I continue to praise and glorify God with every breath to the end, then maybe that is the answer.

With love, —MA

Chapter Ten

Life into Life

Nay, but as when one layeth
His worn-out robes away,
And, taking new ones, sayeth,
"These will I wear today!"
So putteth by the soul
Lightly its garb of flesh,
And passeth to inherit
A residence afresh.

—Bhagavad Gita (2:22)

This morning I awoke early, went out into the living room, and sat down. Looking out the large expanse of glass in the sliding doors, I realized what an unusually beautiful day it was. I opened a slider, stepped out onto the deck, and breathed deeply of the cold, brisk, fresh air. A thankful prayer, seemingly always there, burst from my lips as I greeted the morning in song. The approach of winter felt good—a promise of rest in this ever-changing forest.

Refreshed, I went back in and sat down. Before me were poems written by our dear friend, Victor Steinman, who had just died of cancer. I picked up the poems and began to read them to myself. I was so engrossed in the agony, and yet undying hope, expressed in his poems that I lost myself in them, and was filled with grief. I could feel his pain, his strength, and then . . . I remembered his final defeat.

WATCH OUT WORLD

Watch out World: Here I come!
You can throw your best punches at me,
But if you don't kill me
I'll be back stronger and better!

Is that all you've got:
A few diseases, broken bones,
Mean people, washed-up jobs,
Grief, failure, broken hearts,
Shame, misery, fire, brimstone,
And apocalyptic rumblings. . . .

Is that all you've got!
Well that's nothing,
Because you have no idea
Who I truly am. . . .
I tell you now
That I am a Mighty Flame
Of the Great Cosmic Fire of Being.
The very fire that powers the sun and the stars . . .
That fire powers me!

So watch out World: Here I come!
Believe me . . . you're in big trouble,
Because you messed with the wrong dude
And I'm breathing Fire!
So watch out world: Here I come!

When I finished reading this dramatic poem of Victor's, there was a sudden, overwhelming fragrance of flowers, profound and penetrating. I stood up, sensed the surrounding area, and felt a presence. I knew it was Vic. I was filled with emotion. I hurried down to the bedroom, where George was meditating. I said, "George, I was just reading Vic's poetry, and I smell flowers, and Vic is here!," at which point I broke down crying, remembering his sufferings.

"Saint Ta, your friend was not defeated."

"Oh, Sweet Jesus, thank you for telling me that."

* * *

Vic was a very special person—a true friend of George and mine. He lived at the Retreat and groomed the trails. He was a psychologist and would often counsel guests while walking with them in the forest.

After his cancer really took hold, he decided to finally go West to be with family for his last days on earth. He gave away all of his earthly possessions, which were very few. When I picked Vic up to take him to Grand Rapids to catch his flight west, all he had in his possession were two small bags, one empty—made of cloth. On the way to the airport, he wanted to talk about dying, the after-life, relaxation, breath work and other things important to him. During the trip, Spirit helped me answer the many questions he had.

As I waited with him in the crowded airport, a large black woman, laden with jewels and some baggage, with an entourage of people flitting about her, stood right in front of Vic. There was no room for her to sit and little room to stand. I was impressed by the contrast between the woman and Vic. He was shining as he sat, embracing his heart, unaware of the picture they posed while she stood nearly knee to knee with him in all her jewels. My heart went out to him. When he had to board the plane, there was a hard, sudden letting go. We would never see each other again in these physical forms.

When I returned to my car, there was his small cloth bag, with musical impressions painted on it, and I realized it was a gift. I keep music books in it.

I had planned on stopping at a large lumber yard in Grand Rapids, after leaving Vic, with the hope that they would have outside lights appropriate for our new garage, at a reasonable price. I really didn't think I would find anything special within our budget. Yet, I found beautiful, large, outside lamps that perfectly matched the color of the siding on our house. They were selling them out. They only had two, just what I needed, ten dollars each. I felt sure that helping Vic when he needed it brought this added blessing. Thank you, Vic.

"Giving of oneself and not asking for anything in return opens the door for receiving. All that anyone does is remembered. In some way, all that is good is rewarded."

"So many people are afraid to die."

"As you die, so shall you live. There is no death, only life. What is raised is imperishable. People are afraid of dying because they are uncertain as to what they will find when they die, or they are afraid of the process. This is not a subject that should be hidden or even kept from children, nor should it be dwelt on. Most people die with a smile on their face. Ever wonder why? People spend a lot of time worrying about dying, and it is fruitless. Worry can make you physically sick. Do not waste your precious life on uncertainties. Dwell only in the present with love and savor every moment.

"You do not remember how it was to go from the womb to your mother's arms. Your world in the womb, where all your needs were met, was safe and it was all you knew. You did not know there would be life, after life in the womb. Yet in birthing, life to life was given. So also, in this life, you simply pass over into a new life. There is nothing to fear."

"I was near death after surgery, many years ago. I went from my unconscious physical self to full consciousness out of body, watching the doctors' frantic attempts at arousing me. I remember the absolute bliss and the beautiful, pain-free, burdenless state I was in, with no concern for what was going on. I felt drawn to radiant light coming from above, but then the next thing I knew, I was sitting on the edge of the bed in spirit, and I laid myself down into my physical body. I don't even consciously know what drew me back in. All I can say is that I am not afraid of dying any more."

"There were things you needed to do."

"The first time I dealt with death and dying, with a patient, was when I was doing an occupational therapy internship in a sub-acute wing of a hospital. I had a patient who gave the nurses difficulty when it was time for him to get up in the morning. I realized that he loved to eat. So, every morning, I would go into his room, tell him it was time for breakfast, and help him help himself get dressed and finally into his wheelchair for his meal. He was totally unaware that I had just given him occupational therapy treatment in the form of ADL's (activities of daily living). For him it was simply getting out of bed, washing up, and dressing.

"After breakfast, I would take him to the therapy room. He would reluctantly work with me in therapy and yet, time after time, related, 'I don't want to be doing this; I just want to die.' Finally one day, in front of all others in the therapy room, I knelt down in front of him and repeated back to him, out loud, 'So you are telling me you don't want to be doing this; you just want to die.' 'Yes,' he said, 'I just want to die.' All grew quiet in the therapy room as other patients and staff stopped to listen. I asked him, 'So if you just want to die, what is the hold up? . . . Are you afraid?' 'Yes, I have done bad things in my life,' he said. I asked him, 'Are you sorry?' 'Yes.' I asked him, 'Do you believe in God?' 'Yes.' Then I said to him, 'I believe that is all that is necessary. Would you like to talk to a clergy person?' He said, 'Yes.' Arrangements were made for him to see clergy, and it wasn't long after that that he died.

"Another time, while I was working in a nursing home, I was approached by nursing staff to talk to a man who was dying. The social worker was unable to come to work that day, so they picked me. I thought, 'Sure. Why not? No big deal. I can talk to a dying man.'

"When I got to the door of his room, I was stopped in my tracks, and I had to lean against the framework of the door. It was like hitting a wall. I couldn't go through. Suddenly, intuitively, a familiar prayer was on my lips, 'May the words of my mouth and the meditations of my heart be acceptable to you, Oh God.' The wall lifted, and I walked in and sat down alongside the patient's bed. He had tubes coming out of various places on his body and was totally dependent on others for his needs. I picked up his hand, and instantly felt centered and connected to him. I looked at him and said, 'So what do you make of all of this?' I was surprised that those words would come out of my mouth. It wasn't even a comforting thing. It was a blatant question. Yet this man totally opened up and talked to me of his suffering and of his desire to die. 'My family wants me to live. Do you think it would be all right if I die? I want to die.'

"Oh my . . . here he was, wanting to die, but instead hanging on because his family didn't want him to die. His family was keeping him from passing over. He was asking me if it was okay to die!"

"Many circumstances can keep a person from dying. Thought forms, desires, family and loved ones, and even situations that seemingly need taking care of keep people from letting go, even if they want to die. Family and friends need to be aware of this and allow a letting go, so the passing is easier for their loved one. Even after a loved one dies, there is sometimes a holding on to their memory,

keeping the loved one's spirit near, and confused, and unable to go to the light. Let them go and let God. . . . It is an act of love. There is nothing to fear for the dying or the left behind."

"This dying man simply seemed to need someone to talk to who would give him permission that it was okay to die and that everything would be fine. And I gave him that permission. It seemed right."

"It was, Saint Ta."

"It is amazing to me that so much is done for the living and so little for the dying.

"I want to mention another incident, because I want his story to live on.

"I was called in to do an occupational therapy evaluation and to provide treatment for a man who was bedridden. I decided to work with him for a few days, so I could write up a program for the nurses to follow. This gentle man lay in bed, day after day, never able to get out of bed, hanging on. He was a pleasant man, who didn't have the strength to hold a conversation. I would move his limbs and chat with him, even though I didn't get much response from him. He would smile and just be very sweet.

"One day, out of the blue, he weakly whispered to me, 'I think . . . I have it . . . all figured out.' I bent over him to hear him better and asked, 'What did you say?' He slowly repeated, 'I think . . . I have it . . . all figured out.' Curious, I asked, as I bent even closer to him, 'What is it that you have figured out?' And he answered, 'Why . . . I am . . . still alive.' I looked into his eyes and softly asked, 'And why do you think you are still alive?' And he feebly said, 'I think . . . it's because . . . God still . . . has something . . . for me to do.'

"This was an absolutely profound statement from a man lying there, unable to perform any kind of bodily functions on his own, tube-fed, barely able to speak. Here he was, just lying there, day after day . . . and he feels he is still alive because God still wants him to do something! Amazed, I asked him, 'What do you think it is that God wants you to do?' He answered, 'I don't know. . . . Maybe it's simply . . . to say . . . some kind word . . . to a nurse aide . . . to make her day.' Oh . . . I was filled with love and awe for this dying man. As he talked to me, he shared he was ready to go any time.

"Then I saw you, Jesus, taking on this man's pain. His smile was radiant. His whole body appeared to be melting into you, as if a great weight had been lifted. And, yes, he did have something to do. By staying alive long enough to tell me he thought God wanted him to do something, he made it possible for me to tell his story and let others know of his beautiful perseverance.

"I have shared his story with many people who felt helpless and hopeless and wanted to die, even when they had a lot of life left in them. It often helps them realize that, yes, God does have something for them to live for, something to do, no matter how little it seems or how futile things appear."

"Saint Ta, what loveliness radiates from you when you talk of these beautiful experiences. His work lives on in your remembrance and sharing."

"I learned, several years ago, a procedure called 'sacred act of release.' It is a technique performed for a person suffering in their last days, and having difficulty passing over. This is done with prayers to God for the person's highest good. The person is not touched and there is only initial conversation to seek his or her acceptance. And, any time I have ever used it, they have passed on within a few hours, or at the most, within a day. In some hospitals, nurses would ask me to help those that were having difficulty passing over. I have an instant, intuitive feeling as to whom to work with.

"This sacred act of release is always profound. For me to be with someone who is dying is a blessed time, an honor."

"Saint Ta, it is rare for a person to have this gift. It can only be done with unconditional love, purity, and through the guidance and will of God. This gift allows releases of the hold this life has upon the person, and that hold is mighty. With each release, even further releases are allowed to happen, including passing over. It is with blessings from God that you are able to do this. I cannot express to you, in a language you will understand, how loving an act this is that you do."

"Why is it that I am only moved to help some people and not others to pass over?"

"Partly because of your knowledge of death and dying issues. You are fully aware of whether a person is dying or not. You are simply moved to help them let it all go. Intellectually, you know the signs. Intuitively, you know their soul."

"Jesus, I want to ask a question about another experience I was never quite sure of. I was in a nursing home, working, and I was drawn to go into the room of a resident who was not a patient of mine. There were many nurses in the room and a lot of commotion. As I walked in, someone told me an ambulance had been called. There was a man lying in bed—dying. He was very afraid. When the nurses saw me come in, they left me alone with him. They knew that I would often be available for comforting and helping dying patients. I walked up to his bed, took his hand and laid my other hand on his heart to relax him, and started to talk to him. 'Don't be afraid,' I said, 'It's okay. God is a loving God. He is a forgiving God. Passing over is very beautiful because I died once and I know how wonderful it is. When you see the light, let yourself go and go to the light.'

"I explained to him, 'When I died, the most important thing I remember is the beautiful, peaceful feeling I had. I was no longer aware of sorrow or pain. Yet I was conscious of all that was happening. I was fully aware. All the burdens, pains, cares and worries were gone. Nothing heavy remained to weigh me down anymore. There was nothing to fear. I felt as if I were spirit, loving it completely in ecstatic joy. I cannot even come close to explaining this in its totality. In giving myself up, I was being given new life, not death. I felt drawn to a light, cascading down at me from above. As I experienced a great longing, I reached for it.' All of this I told this dying man, and he became comforted. However, he did not die until after the ambulance came and took him away.

"After I left work, later in the afternoon, I went to a pottery shop. The owner of the shop walked up to me and asked, 'Ah, what is that fragrance you are wearing? It is so beautiful! It smells like gardenias!' She kept sniffing all around me, smelling the fragrance. I told her, 'I'm not wearing anything' and 'I can't smell anything.' She said, 'Oh, Yes! You must be. It smells like gardenias! It is wonderful!' And she walked ever-closer and said to me, 'It's your breath!' I immediately thought of the dying man and knew that he had passed on.

"Sweet Jesus, was this the breath of God?"

Strange how I ask questions, knowing full-well the answers. Jesus must want the questions asked so the answers can be written.

"Out of expanded awareness, you are able to experience the breath of the omnipresent God. In this instance, it was someone else that needed to experience God's fragrant, healing breath through you."

"While I was working in Carlsbad, I received a phone call from my birth-brother, Doug. I had not lived with my birth-siblings after I was given away at the age of two. I always knew my sisters and brothers existed, but it's only since we got older that we have been able to see each other more.

"Doug was calling to tell me of our brother, Jim, who was comatose and dying. The doctors wanted the family to pull the plug, so to speak. Doug was beside himself and didn't know what to do. From what he told me of Jim's condition, I felt it would be the right thing to do. I did call the hospital and my mind was not changed.

"A week went by, then the phone rang again. This time, Doug had the same story and his voice had a tone of desperation. I felt a strong sense of urgency to see Jim. So, unthinkingly, I said to Doug, 'I'll see you tomorrow.' I was in Carlsbad, New Mexico, and Jim was in a hospital in Detroit! I got on the phone and was able to get a flight, and arrived in Detroit the following evening, just as I knew I would.

"Jim was always a happy-go-lucky person, from the little I knew of him, never married and never settled, lovable and kind to everyone. I remember, when I was a teenager, Jim came to visit me at my foster-family home, traveling across state on a bicycle. He was one year younger than myself and didn't really have a home. He just went from one relative to another, long enough to get some attention and food. Then off he would go to another relative's home.

"I loaned him a flannel shirt while he was with us. Years later he sent me the shirt in the mail! Here he was, nearly always down and out, and he was sending a shirt back to me!

"Doug picked me up at the airport and drove me to the hospital. I entered Jim's room. He was hooked up to everything and was comatose. I centered myself, attempting to get over the shock of seeing Jim in this condition. As Doug and I stood on opposite sides of Jim's bed, I scanned his body and found chaos in his energy field at his forehead, heart area and his right hip. I don't know why I did what followed. All I know is, I was moved to ask Doug to watch the heart rate monitor. I placed my hands over Jim's body and began going in a clock-wise circle over his heart. I started to talk to him about dying. I told him, in heart talk, that God is a loving God and a forgiving God, that there was nothing to be afraid of, to just let go and go to the light, and God would take care of him. The heart-rate monitor went up twenty beats while I stood alongside of his bed. I knew, from the increase in heartbeats, that he knew I was there. He could hear me speaking to him in heart talk and sense me.

"Then the doctors wanted to talk to Doug and me, so we left the room. I told the doctors what I found when I scanned Jim, and they did not even flinch but said to me, 'You can feel the chaos in the forehead because he is having seizures, in the heart area because his heart is failing, and in the hip area because that is how high the gangrene is.'

"We went back into Jim's room and, again, I asked Doug to watch the heart-rate monitor. Again, I placed my hand over Jim's heart and, in heart talk, reassured him that God is a loving, forgiving God and that, for once, someone else would take care of him and that he could relax now. Again, the heart-rate went up twenty beats. Again, I knew he was aware of what I was saying and that I was there. While Doug stood at the bedside, I performed the sacred act of release, totally feeling oneness with Jim and God in an energy of love.

"The room grew quiet and the energy softened as Jim died within minutes, ventilator and all else still going. What a blessed honor it was to be there.

"Even though I had to leave before the actual funeral, I helped plan his funeral. And I learned so much more about Jim. He had lived with my brother, Doug, but also had a room in downtown Detroit. Apparently he would often feed the street people downtown. They knew that, when pay-day came, Jim would cook them up a feast and was always good for a hand-out. Jim also kept a coin jar in his room and, every time it would fill up, someone would steal it. Jim continued to put coins in the jar. When it came time for the funeral to start, they had to hold it up because the street people were trying to get transportation to the funeral."

* * *

"When a person dies, can they take time-out to rest for a while before reincarnating? Is that possible?"

"Yes."

"How long would this time-out be experienced?"

"In the irrelevancy of time of the after-world, there would be no definite experience of length of time."

"So then, would it be possible that, if I died and wanted to wait for my husband, it might seem only seconds before he came to me."

"Yes. However, if you so desire to have your loved ones with you, then you are not yet ready to give it all up to go to God. Still, if you so desire to have a loved one with you, you will surely manifest it and you shall, eventually, simply reincarnate to continue your growth toward God.

"However, truly I say to you, learn to be self-sufficient. Do not depend so on others, including loved ones. Learn to

love thy self. Truly there is nothing you can take to God except that which is deeply embedded into your soul. Therefore I tell you, you must give up all attachments. I do not mean you should not have, while on earth, but only that you should not need so strongly that you cannot give up your possessions or a loved one to go to God."

"So, we might desire time-out with a loved one and reincarnation, or we are liberated to simply go to God?"

"Yes."

"What form would we take on in time-out?"

"In God's likeness, as a subtle body, with limited realizations, and yet with full consciousness of self and surroundings."

"That sounds like how it is for us now. Is it all pleasant?"

"It is what you make of it."

"How is our aura connected to our soul?"

"At the end of each lifetime, the soul assimilates your auric energy in the form of varying degrees of light as love. Your soul is your self-identification. Your soul is within and without you, seemingly caged as a bird of paradise, held at bay by your karmic desires, attachments and ego within the physical, astral, or causal levels and planes. Still, the soul is oneness with self and with all creation, reciprocally.

"Reincarnating back to earth or to different planes gives you the chance to eliminate self-perceived karma, desires and ego. The more light and love your soul absorbs from

each lifetime, the closer the soul advances to final absorption into the non-dualistic, highest heavenly consciousness with God."

"Tell us about the different levels of afterlife?"

"Every person is at a different level of spiritual attainment. When you pass over, there are limitless levels of hell and varying lower levels of heaven, each befitting the individual. The plane you go to when you pass over depends on your state of spiritual consciousness."

"What do you mean by planes, or levels of heaven?"

"There is so much more to the spiritual levels and planes than you can ever imagine. It is so vast that even your best visionary could not envision the totality of it. It is not something that can be learned in books or found under a microscope. As I speak simply, I can only will that you will understand."

"I read about the physical, astral and causal bodies, and then there are earth, astral and causal planes. What is the difference?"

"The physical, astral and causal bodies are a part of you while earthbound. The earth, astral and causal planes are your dwelling places while on your spiritual path to God.

"The astral body is so much more than the chemistry of the physical body. It is the subtle body of everything about you that is not chemical: life energy, feelings, emotions, intelligence, senses and more. The astral body dwells, reciprocally, within your physical body and causal body.

"The causal body is of and beyond thought as you know it. It, too, dwells reciprocally, within your physical body and astral body. An advanced soul may realize, through the causal body, perception beyond what the five senses allow and materializations of desires, through thought alone, while still in the dualistic physical realm.

"Desires, karma and all forms of ego confine one's soul within the physical, astral and causal bodies and planes and can keep you from experiencing ever-higher states of grace.

"As I said before, when you pass over and shed the physical body, you may, in your subtle astral body, go into the astral plane, a state of consciousness, where limitless levels of hell and limitless lower levels of heaven exist. Some call the astral plane purgatory. Within the astral plane, in the varying heavens, there are desires that are ever-more difficult to overcome because of their more-wondrous nature. It is much easier to rid oneself of desires while in the physical plane than when you reach the bea-tific astral or creator-like causal state."

George was sitting nearby while I waited for Jesus to tell me of the causal plane. I was so confused by what came that I was moved to go inward to try to feel what Jesus was saying. Stepping through the veils, I was in the causal plane. I began to explain out loud to George what I was ex-periencing:

"There is no body . . . no sense of being in a body. I am attempting to look at myself . . . and there is nothing to see but . . . all pervading sense of light, love, silence and joy. . . . I am one with the all. . . . There are no flowers, nor trees, nor anything material. . . . I still have awareness . . . of seemingly-expanded senses and thought energy. . . . I feel I could materialize flowers if I wanted to. . . . I realize there are other souls nearby. . . . Activity is taking place . . . directed at helping on the earth plane . . . astral plane . . . and elsewhere in the universe. Distance and time don't seem to exist. . . . I imagine they could selflessly answer prayers . . . be at the side of the sick in body, mind and spirit . . . and reach out to instill love . . . into masses of people . . . situations . . . and all of creation."

Later, Jesus addressed this vision. *"In the bliss and wondrous nature of the causal plane, you may want to dwell there forever. Further, imagine if you will, Saint Ta, that it is here that the choirs of angels begin. One hears them with the soul senses and expanded love, and the bliss is beyond words."*

"I often said I would like to sing in the heavenly choir!"

I could not imagine hearing the angels. I tried to quiet myself. I put my hands on my face, and bowed my head, and tried to quiet my thoughts and drown out noises. The tinnitus, ringing in my ears, wouldn't go away. Jesus whispered to me, *"Listen with your heart, not with your ears. There are no ears in the causal world."* I went into my heart and my breathing slowed. Still, I wasn't receptive enough. Jesus' whispers reverberated within me, *"Expand your senses. Listen with your soul."* I folded in upon myself. *"Expand your love."* My breathing became as if nothing and the tinnitus quieted. Nothing existed except heavenly music beyond anything I had ever heard. . . . I sensed it in ways beyond ordinary hearing. . . .

Jesus brought me back suddenly and, seemingly out of context, said, *"Still, if one should fall from grace within the causal plane, the soul is banished to, or self-imposes, a fall through the veils, back to their beginnings. This fall is less traumatic if self-imposed, but grievously more traumatic if one is banished, and both take many lifetimes to recover from."*

I gasped at this thought. I cannot even imagine how that must be. My mind could not fathom it in its totality. . . . I reeled from the abrupt change in emotions from choirs of angels to envisioning a sudden darkness. Joy came to me then, as if I needed it, and I wondered what would keep my soul from going from the causal plane to final absorption into God. Then the realization came to me that it was desire to remain in the causal plane, along with subtle ego, as the thought of being separate from God instead of being one with God, and of being the doer of good actions, that would keep one in the causal plane, just as more-gross forms of ego keep one on earth or on the astral plane. Even in this blissful, joyful causal plane, if we continue to have desires, identify ourselves as separate from God, or identify with the good that we do, this stays us from the highest heaven with God. We must learn to surrender our desires and identity to God and, in that surrender, all forms of ego will evaporate. Truly the last thing to go is ego.

"Once you can release yourself of every desire, experience the oneness above and beyond the perceived dualism of all the realms, and surrender the self, only then will your

soul be one with God, for unless a soul be perfected, one cannot enter the highest heaven with God."

Questioning further, I asked, "When liberated, is all sense of self gone? Is there still self?"

"How would you know you were in paradise if there was no awareness. However, this awareness is without dualism, or distinctive separations. All is truly unified as one, as the great I AM, and within this paradise you dwell as pure, egoless soul, forever, with God."

"Is it possible to go from our earthly home direct to the highest heaven with God?"

"Since God is everywhere and God is in heaven, you must realize this highest heaven is a state of consciousness. Heaven is not a place in time. Truly I say unto you, thou shalt dwell in the house of the Lord when you become self-realized, without the limitations of the ego, even while embracing life on earth or in the astral or causal plane. In God's house there are many mansions, each mansion a state of heavenly consciousness."

"You say we must be free of all desires, yet, isn't my desiring to be free from all desires also a desire that keeps my soul continually caged? How can I break from this prison to be free?"

"Your desire to go to God is, in part, your state of consciousness with God's love and presence already in you. Detach your self from this desire and embrace the truth. You do not have to go to God. God is already within.

"Eliminate all attachment to desires. This does not

mean that you cannot have possessions and pretty things and family and work and fun. It means simply that you shouldn't be so attached to possessions that they would interfere with your spiritual progress and that you couldn't easily let them go.

"You came to earth to perform certain work. Yet, do not become attached to the books you will write. Simply write, send them off, and they will be fruitful. Then share the bounty . . . with love and joy.

"God's non-dualistic, highest heaven is a state of consciousness where there is simply love in all its splendorous oneness with God. Surrender your separateness from God. You do not have to die to experience and embrace the realization that all things are unified in love and that there is nothing to compare to, even while living in a world of perceived dualism."

"You mean I really could skip the astral plane and the causal plane, where advanced souls go, and be with God while on earth? This sounds like monopoly."

Smiling, Jesus said, *"Yes. And, hardly!"*

Laughing, I continued, "So we could choose to simply be with God."

"Only when there are no karmic debts or desires, including attachments to those gone before you, and your ego is released, will your soul be advanced enough to realize that heaven is within. Reincarnating or staying in the heavens will be of little comparison."

"So, you are saying that, if someone's soul is advanced

enough to be self-realized, it would make no difference where they are?"

"*Yes. Still, when you become one with God, there is growth and learning, whether it is here on earth, another plane, or with God in the highest state of heavenly consciousness. Learning never stops. God is limitless. Heaven is within and without. Heaven is everywhere and everything. Even with God, there is growth and ever-higher states of heaven, wherein creation is ongoing, unlimited, beyond dualism.*"

"If we reach the final absorption in the highest state of heavenly consciousness, do we ever come back to earth?"

"*In surrendering your self to God and becoming as one with the great I AM, you give up your whole self to God. Even so, God may determine your soul may be needed back on earth, and, if so, it is very possible to reincarnate to earth as a liberated, egoless soul.*"

"So . . . what of hell?"

"*If you are unable to forgive yourself and others, when you pass over you will surely create a perceived hell fitting for you.*"

"I remember, last spring, the thought of dying felt very comforting. The feeling lasted a full week. There weren't any perceived upsets in my life at all. I wasn't depressed. I simply felt a deep longing for God. If it wasn't for my husband and family, I probably would have let go. It felt as easy as it is to let go and fall asleep at night.

"Then, later that week, I had just dressed for the Sunday

service when I was drawn to the bedroom window. I was mesmerized by the swaying of the tall trees in the wind. The branches danced and flowed, slowly, back and forth. As I watched the trees swaying, I felt a strong pull to God drawing me ever closer. My movements began to reflect the dance of the trees. I felt melded with the movement. I became shades of brilliant green, and then light, and flowed on the wind amongst the leaves. It was beautiful. There was no body. I knew God and I were one. I was lost in it. Then I suddenly felt grieved, battling whether to go or stay. I remembered how it felt to have died once before. The longing for that peace was immense. I felt no fear. There was only peace, quiet, and timelessness. Then a feeling of incompletion came over me, and I wiped away the tears. It was time to leave for the service, and I regained my composure so I wouldn't upset George. Why am I experiencing this?"

"What are you afraid of?"

"There was no fear for myself, just for leaving my family."

"This was a resurrection into a new consciousness. You are resurrected daily, as you die daily. You are more fully aware of this daily resurrection in your breath work. You have made many profound changes in your lifetime, which were steps on the path toward the highest goal. Your work is still being done. Life, even on earth, is a gift. Savor it moment by moment."

"I saw life, all along, as a gift. The beauty and the

veiled. The pain and the joy. The laughter and the tears. The grief and the lessons. All gifts.

"Sweet Jesus, you speak to me through my days and nights. You are within my heart. You are my friend. I love you. I wish everyone could feel Your love. They would never be alone."

"Love is for all creation. All people are important to me and to God. No matter what a person has done, love is there, unconditionally. It is as simple as that. There is nothing more to know."

"For those who are not yet realized, what if they mess their life up? Will this set them back?"

"They have lifetimes to work on it. Each lifetime builds upon the others. Listen when I say . . . where you are is where you will find what you must work on. Watch your ego. Your ego will alert you to what you have to work on. If you find life too difficult, you should begin today to advance your spiritual life. Sincerely forgive yourselves and others, so that those seemingly-unforgivable acts will not lead to karmic debt that will have to be worked out in another lifetime."

"What about those who enjoy their lives the way they are. Might they want to just reincarnate over and over the way they are?"

"First of all, they will not reincarnate in the same place or with the same personality. There will be different situations for dealing with their chosen karma. Still, somewhere along the way, they will catch a glimpse of heaven, and will

realize what they have been missing and want more and more of it. You do not lose spiritual advancement from one life to another. For how could your soul forget the bliss, as you grow in remembrance of God?

"Do you remember the parable about the laborers in the vineyard who were hired throughout the day, and yet at the end of the day, received equal pay. So it is with anyone along their path. The kingdom of heaven is within anyone's reach, even in the last breath."

"I love that parable. What is interesting is that those hired first grumbled about those hired last receiving the same pay. I guess I could understand that I might feel the same way. And yet, if I knew that the payoff would be awareness of God, I would rejoice for those who finally realized that, whether they came before or after me.

"I love that we don't lose what we have spiritually gained, however little it might be?"

"You don't lose."

"Aren't you going to elaborate?"

"Do I have to?"

"You are playing with me again. This whole thing sounds like a game: Take two steps forward and one back. Yet you say each life builds learning experiences for the advancement of our soul."

"Yes. But don't look at it as if you would take steps back. You simply start over to address karmic debt. Each life holds what your soul needs for your spiritual evolution."

"What about those who commit suicide?"

"They reincarnate to work off that karma. All is not lost."

"What about those who have or perform abortions?"

"There are so many individual situations that warrant or censure abortion. Even the fetus has his or her own karma, or is sent to intervene in the karma of the people involved, in ways unfathomable by the human mind. You cannot kill what cannot die. The soul lives on, life after life. Therefore, it is not for me to say to one, it is right, and to another, it is wrong. It is not for me nor you to judge. And, even when God intervenes, it is with love and guidance, without judgment. Life is precious, before birth and after birth. Life is precious, before war and after war. Do you condemn those who send your youth to die in war? Within your dualistic world, you perceive circumstances that warrant war, even as you perceive circumstances that warrant abortion. Therefore, I simply ask that whatever you do, do it with love.

"God loves everyone, not just the saintly. It saddens God and I that some of you who are or have been involved in abortion have feelings of guilt that affects your lives. You bury parts of the memory within layers of veil, and wonder why you experience stresses. Memories continue to surface, reminding you of the experience and of your feelings of guilt. I say to you, wrap your self with the love of God, forgive your self and others, come to terms with your feelings, and go on.

"If you aren't able to allow yourself to feel the love of

God, I offer myself for you. I love you. I am here to bear your burdens, your sadness, and your feelings of guilt. Unburden your self onto me; then live and heal in each present moment, with love and with no concern over the past."

There was a slight hesitation of time within a beautiful, sweet moment of bliss. It brought me to tears thinking of Jesus relieving everyone of their burdens, if only they would go to Him. It lifted my love for Him to ever-new heights.

"Ah, Sweet Jesus, You are so dear to me. . . .

"I feel your palm as I lie down within it,
soft and warm upon my joyful face.
I feel your arms around me, softly gathered,
keeping me safe within your healing grace. . . ."

* * *

"Sweet Jesus, is there ever a form of punishment?"

"God does not punish."

"You mean, all the time I was growing up, what I was told, 'If you aren't good, God will punish you,' is wrong?"

"As I have said before, with your free will, you are the judge. All of your life, in your self-judging, you have been hard on yourselves. You must love and forgive yourself, so your soul can be relieved from burden. You are your soul."

"Our soul carries burdens?"

"The soul carries karmic burdens in the form of darkness."

"How can we rid ourselves of this darkness?"

"The darkness can only be diminished or eliminated by your free will. No one else can take away your darkness; you must do that yourself. If someone were to simply take away your darkness, you would die a final death, with no chance to address what is lost.

"Your soul is freed from darkness and the light of your soul increases as you live in love, forgiving self and others, and eliminate desires. When your soul is finally free of darkness, your soul will be pure light.

"As I said many times, I came to free the sins of all through the message of truth and love. My life and death offers this perfection for all time, through forgiveness of all past karmic debt, for those who listen to the truth and live in love. Still it is up to you, using your own free will, to accept this truth and free your soul. As I said before, unless a soul be perfected, one cannot enter the highest heaven, into final absorption with God."

"Can other masters eliminate my karma?"

"Woe to those who claim false promises. Your free will prevents even me from eliminating your karma until you have chosen belief and understanding. You must be spiritually ready in heart and mind to understand and accept an offer of freedom from sin. Through the Father, who loves you, I can only offer freedom with your acceptance. Simple words of deep love, and actions of love may display your understanding and free your soul of its darkness. And then, and only then, when you ask shall your karma be taken from you."

"When I am in the present moment and at one with all creation, I feel as if I am not a part of the physical world. Is there karma in that state?"

"Saint Ta, you are in the world but not of the world when you are in this consciousness. Karma is too empha-sized. Good karma exists also, and in that state, good karma is evident."

After a time of reflection . . . "Sweet Jesus, I read about a punishing God in the Bible, in the Old Testament. Now you speak of a loving God who doesn't judge. Why has it changed?"

"Biblical history can be interpreted to reflect to each of you a God that fits for where you are in your spiritual awareness.

"People living during Old Testament history created a God in their minds and hearts that would bring people into obeisance with strong language and action that they could understand. They coveted a God who was judgmental. They created what they believed they needed. They wrote laws to reflect these beliefs.

"If you are at a lesser spiritual awareness, and need a God of vengeance to support your anger and judgmental nature, you would interpret God as vengeful. You must re-member, what you sow, you reap.

"From a higher spiritual awareness, you would want a God of love and mercy, and you interpret God as loving and merciful.

"I was sent to earth to show you a loving God. In the New Testament you will find this loving God. There is no

room for vengeance where there is LOVE.

"This truth is often laid aside or misinterpreted. The One Truth is . . . such great love has the omnipresent Father for you, that whosoever believes in Him shall not perish but shall have everlasting life."

"Does anyone ever really lose?"

"No. God is a loving God, who bestows upon all the gift of life, to start over and over, daily and through reincarnation, until you conquer karmic debt and gain life everlasting in heaven, never to perish. Wherein lies the vengeance?"

* * *

Today was a beautiful, sunny day, but cold. Now in the early evening, as I look out our sliding glass doors, I see barren tree branches and a soft blanket of snow on the ground, and I think of the wintergreen which keeps its dark-green color all winter long under the snow. I see soaring evergreen trees and the blue, blue sky. The deep, bright colors, in harmony with white snow, remind me once again of Mother Nature as the perfect color coordinator.

The whole forest is ready for the winter, yet still full of life. The deer come to eat the last of the clover in the yard. Pawing through the light snow, they find it easily. The chickadees stay here for the winter. They brave the cold with us and brighten our days. The squirrels, in their comical mannerisms, constantly seek food to stash away in secret places, never seeming to get enough. I truly think they forget where they put everything.

George and I were eating our dinner when we started

talking about my present one-day-a-week job as an occupational therapist at a rehabilitation center, where I cannot talk of my spiritual experiences. I said to him that, here at the Retreat, I am more comfortable about sharing healings and experiences. In the everyday world, many people have to keep these things secret within their heart, for fear of ridicule.

George then reminded me of a passage in the Bible, where Jesus said, "You are the light of the world. A city set on a hill cannot be hid. Nor do men light a lamp and put it under a bushel, but on a stand, and it gives light to all in the house. Let your light so shine before men, that they may see your good works and give glory to your Father who is in heaven."

I said to George, "I wish Jesus had said that" . . . then, before I could add, "to me for the book.", Jesus was right there, saying, *"I did."*

Later, feeling the presence of Jesus next to me, I said to Him, "Jesus, I feel such love flowing from Your every word. I would like to go on and on for I know our conversations will never cease, and yet I feel I need to find closure for now. I can only pray that whatever it was You might have wanted readers to realize has been expressed in the book.

"If there is anything more that You want, what would it be?"

There was silence, nothing forthcoming. My tinnitus stopped ringing. All noise ceased. I moved and no sound came forth. I clapped my hands and no sound came forth. I was not afraid. I sat in the silence, pure silence. In timelessness, I felt moved to pray to Jesus, to God, to Spirit, to the One. The sound of my voice was the only sound.

Aloud I prayed: "Oh God, You are the essence of pure love. You are the beacon of light that guides me through rough waters. You are the love on wings of doves every-where. You are my sunset and sunrise. You are my bird song. You are the spring buds, and the falling leaves, and the glistening snow. You are the wave in the ocean and the drop of water. You are the poppy seed. You are the friend, child, husband, father, and mother. You are the sick and in-jured. You are in my heart, always sustaining me with song. There is nothing you need because you are all. Thank you, Oh God, for your presence in my life. Amen."

And then the prayer came back to me in a hushed whis-per, as if it was for everyone, everywhere. . . .

"You are the essence of pure love. You are the beacon of light that guides you through rough waters. You are the love on wings of doves everywhere. You are the sunset and sun-rise. You are the bird song. You are the spring buds, and the falling leaves, and the glistening snow. You are the wave in the ocean and the drop of water. You are the poppy seed. You are the friend, child, wife, father, and mother. You are the sick and injured. You are as a sun-ray of song. There is nothing you need because you are one with all."

And the sounds of everyday life resumed. . . .

Index

Healing Touch, 139, 142,
151-152, 163
Holoenergetics, 106, 162
Kinesiology, 163
Laying on of hands, 57,
107, 148, 154, 156
sacred act of release, 260, 264
self, 143- 144, 150
skeptics, 141-143, 152,
souls, 165
study, 138-139, 162
taking on burdens, 167-168
with love, 106, 162
heart talk, 3, 9, 85-86-87, 264
heaven, 185, 267-268
highest heaven, 270-273, 279
kingdom of, 47, 276
mansion, 271
on earth, 66, 118, 122, 125,
167
treasures, 121,
within, 166, 185, 273
hell, 174, 167, 268, 273
perception of, 273
purgatory , 268
highest good, 36, 134, 234, 260
homosexuality, *see* gay rights
honesty, 71, *see also* truth
hope, 11, 115. 120
hopelessness, 158,
humanity, 66, 104, 112, 115,
119-120, 126, 166

I AM,
imperfection, *see* perfection
incarnation, *see* reincarnation
imagination, *see* creativity
inequality, 115-116-118
infirmed, 57, 145, 148, 245
innerchild, *see* child
inner self, 53, 62
insects, 84-85, 99
intelligence, 74, 82, 166

intention, 73, 96, 106-107, 142,
169-172, 226, 231, 233, 241
intuition, 52, 71-73, 96, 134,
136, 139, 164-165, 224, 234
see also God, as guide

Jealousy, 119
Jesus
appearance, 2, 7-9, 36-38
bear burdens, 278
Christed incarnation of God,
35, 178
cleansing the church, 180
cross, 177-178
forgiveness, 177
freeing sin, 177, 178
giving of Himself, 277-278
guidance, 8, 138, 211
life and death, 177-178, 279
living in love, 178, 215
love, 70, 79, 181, 211, 275
pictures of, 36, 209-211
rebel, 174
resurrection, 178
return, 46-47
sacrifice, 177
sent to earth, 115, 176
Son of God, 33, 245
suffering, 167
super imposed on others, 167
the Way, the Truth, and the
Life, 178
see also Christ Consciousness
joy, 38, 60-61, 67, 167, 176, 187,
225, 237
judgment , 40-42, 68, 125,
175, 177, 182, 205-206, 277
non-judgment, 32, 38-40, 52,
123, 176, 182

karma, definition of, 175-176,
173. 268, 277-279
as reward, 51-52, 162, 175

Books for the Heart and Mind

——*A Course in Miracles,* © Foundation for Inner Peace, 1996.

——*Blessed Souls, Teachings of Karunamayi,* Sri Matrudevi Visvashanti Ashram Trust, 1998.

——*Gospel of Thomas: Annotated & Explained,* Translator: Stevan L. Davies, Skylight Paths Publishing, 2002.

Amritaswarupananda, Swami
Ammachi, A Biography of Mata Amritanandamayi, Mata Amritanandamayi Center, 1994.

Braden, Gregg,
The Isaiah Effect, Harmony Books, 2000
The Divine Matrix, Hay House, 2006.

Brennan, Barbara
Hands of Light: A Guide to Healing Through the Human Energy Field, Bantam Books, 1987.
Light Emerging, Bantam Books, 1993.

Buscaglia, Leo F.,
Love: What Life is All About, Ballantine Books, 1972.

Cameron, Julia,
The Artist's Way, J.P.Putnam's Sons, 1992.
Finding Water, The Art of Perseverance, Penguin Group, 2006.

Carinci, John P.
The Power of Being Different, AuthorHouse, 2005.

Chopra, Deepak,
The Third Jesus: The Christ We Cannot Ignore. Harmony, 2008.

Dante, Alighieri (author), John Ciardi (translator)
The Divine Comedy, NAL Trade, 2003.

Gandhi, Mohandas,
Gandhi an Autobiography, Beacon Press, 1967

Gibran, Kahlil,
Jesus the Son of Man, Alfred A. Knopf, Inc., 1999, © 1928 by Kahlil Gibran.

Green, Glenda,
Love Without End: Jesus Speaks, Spiritis Publishing, 1998.

Hicks, Esther and Jerry,
The Astonishing Power of Emotions, Hay House, 2007.

Ibsen, Henrik,
A Doll's House, translated by William Archer, John W. Lovell Co., 1890.

Johnston, Mary Ann,
Sustained by Faith – Personal Awakening in God, Tatienne Publishing, 2009;
Messages from Jesus - A Dialogue of Love, Tatienne Publishing, 2009.

Kidd, Sue Monk,
The Dance of the Dissident Daughter, HarperOne, 2006.

Lakshmi Devi, Sai Maa,
Petals of Grace, Essential Teaching for Self Mastery,
HIU Press, 2005.

Lao Tsu,
Tao Te Ching, Vintage Books, 1989

Lasko, Leonard,
Healing With Love, Harper Collins, 1992.

Levi,
The Aquarian Gospel of Jesus the Christ, DeVorss Publications, 2003. Original copyright 1907.

Markides, Kriacos C.,
Homage to the Sun, Penguin Group, 1987.
Magus of Strovolos: The Extraordinary World of a Spiritual healer, Penguin Group, 1989.
Riding With the Lion, Penguin Group, 1995.
Fire in the Heart, Penguin Group, 1996.

Merzel, Dennis Genpo,
Big Mind – Big Heart: Finding Your Way, Big Mind Publishing, 2007.

Moore, Thomas,
The Re-enchantment of Everyday Life, Harper Perennial, 1997.

Morgan, Marlo,
Mutant Message Down Under, Harper Collins Publishers, 1994.

Myss, Caroline,
Anatomy of the Spirit, Three Rivers Press, 1996.

Entering the Castle: An Inner Path to God and Your Soul, Free Press, 2007.

Ram Dass,
Still Here: Embracing Aging, Changing, and Dying, Riverhead Trade, 2000.

Riddell, Carol,
The Findhorn Community, The Findhorn Press, 1991.

Redfield, James,
The Celestine Prophecy, Warner Books, 1997.

Saint Teresa,
The Life of Saint Teresa, translated by J.M. Cohen, Penguin Books, 1958.

Schulz, Mona Lisa,
Awakening Intuition, Using Your Mind-Body Network for Insight and Healing, Harmony Books, 1998

Stearn, Jess,
A Prophet in His Own Country, The Story of Young Edgar Cayce, William Morrow and Company, Inc., 1974.

Sutherland, Patricia
Perilous Journey: A Mother's International Quest to Rescue Her Children, New Horizon Press, 2002.

Tolle, Eckhart,
The Power of Now: A Guide to Spiritual Enlightenment, New World Library, 2004.

Walker III, Ethan,
The Mystic Christ, Devi Press, 2003.

Warren, Rick,
Purpose Driven Life: What on Earth Am I Here For?, Zondervan Publishing Company, 2007.

White Eagle,
Spiritual Unfoldment Boxed Set, 1960;
The Quiet Mind, 1998;
The White Eagle Publishing Trust.

Williamson, Marianne,
Everyday Grace, Riverhead Trade, 2004

Yogananda, Paramahansa,
Autobiography of a Yogi, 1999, revised in 1951 by the author;
Whispers from Eternity, 1999, ©*1935;*
The Second Coming of Christ, 2004;
The Yoga of Jesus: Understanding the Hidden Teachings of the Gospels, 2007,
Self-Realization Fellowship Publishers.

Young, Sarah,
Jesus Calling, Enjoying Peace in His Presence, Integrity Publishers, 2004

Zukav, Gary
The Seat of the Soul, Simon & Schuster, 1989.

Also by Mary Ann Johnston

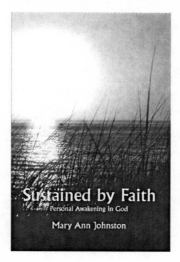

Sustained by Faith

"A powerful story of hope and courage! This book bears witness to the truth that even in the midst of darkness we can be filled with light. Mary Ann candidly and generously shares the details of a difficult life lived in the consciousness of the Holy Presence and in so doing uplifts and inspires us all."

—Marilyn Beker
Senior Screenwriting Professor,
School of Film and Television,
Loyola Marymount University,
Los Angeles, CA

Sustained by Faith is about facing challenges at every step along life's way: abuse, death, transformation, discovery, miracles, purifying and strengthening heart and soul, learning to see clearly and deeply, listening to intuition, and taking chances. You will read of my personal journey, with Jesus' living presence shaping my life through His transforming power of love and kindness, giving me the wisdom to be courageous and to persevere. I hope what I have experienced and learned along the way will be of value to you and that Jesus' words and the support He gave me will touch your heart. And, if this book in some way heals wounds of your own, gives you hope, feeds your meditations, ignites spiritual intuitions from deep within you, or inspires you to be more loving, it will truly have been worth its writing.

—Mary Ann

Learn more at:
www.SustainedbyFaith.com

About the Author

Mary Ann Johnston—author, lecturer, healer and occupational therapist—lives with her husband, George, deep in the forest at Song of the Morning retreat, in the upper part of Lower Michigan. It is from here that she writes of her spiritual life and conversations with Jesus, who came to her as a radiant ethereal being when she was five years old.

In the winter of 1994, while working as a traveling occupational therapist in medical facilities across the country, Mary Ann was made aware that she was able to heal people through the power of Spirit. Her healing gift opened her mind to new horizons. She began to seek solace in meditation and to question her religious upbringing. She realized she had to choose either her church family, which would have stymied her growth as a healer, or the living Christ in her heart. She chose her higher calling.

In 1996, after two years of relying on Spirit to guide her, she was strongly moved by Spirit to study. She now holds many certificates in various healing modalities; however, her healing approach is still the same, as she relies on inner guidance.

Then in 1998, Mary Ann had a profound spiritual awakening, which connected her to higher dimensions of reality, increasing her creativity and awareness of God's graces. She began to write poetry describing the blissful feelings, visions and realizations she was having.

In 2002, Jesus encouraged her to write books, sharing her experiences and his messages of hope and love with all people, everywhere. Her relationship with Jesus was no longer just for her, but for everyone who is searching for answers. Mary Ann receives continuous encouragement from Jesus, who refreshes and supports her through fragrances and blissful energies, through his divine presence and through his counsel.

Mary Ann is also a singer and musician. She has a degree in occupational therapy from Western Michigan University. She teaches workshops, and has been a guest speaker for community groups and churches in many cities around the country and at Song of the Morning.

Her spiritual autobiography, *Sustained by Faith – Personal Awakening in God,* serves as a prelude to this book. She is currently writing a third book.

For additional information about Mary Ann Johnston's healing work, lectures, counseling, and writings, to visit her blog, to be on her mailing list, or for a short bio of George, please visit: http://www.MessagesfromJesus.com

CPSIA information can be obtained
at www.ICGtesting.com
Printed in the USA
FFOW03n1120280218
45320863-45990FF